"The books of Walter Hard present a likeness of a land and its people that deserves a place in the gallery of the best that has been done by the regionalists of the earth. I treasure and reread his volumes."

—Carl Sandburg

"He describes the qualities of Vermonters which continue to survive—honesty and frugality, yes—but always blended with an uncanny sense of humor."

—Madeleine M. Kunin

"Here is a book of poems that should not be regarded as poems. It is a collection of character sketches and stories expressing the humor, pathos and human understanding of the country people of Vermont as no other has been able to do."

The Christian Science Monitor

"In my travels as oral history consultant, from coast to coast I have heard praise of Walter Hard's verses from people with no other contacts with Vermont. This shows his talent for depicting universal humanity in his mountain village."

—Charles T. Morrissey,
Author of *Vermont, A Bicentennial History*

Walter Hard's

VERMONT PEOPLE

Books by Walter Hard

SOME VERMONTERS

SALT OF VERMONT

MOUNTAIN TOWNSHIP

VERMONT VINTAGE

VERMONT VALLEY

VERMONT SALT AND VINTAGE
(Combining *Salt Of Vermont* and *Vermont Vintage*)

THE CONNECTICUT
(Rivers of America Series)

A MATTER OF FIFTY HOUSES

VERMONT NEIGHBORS

VERMONT SAMPLER

THIS IS VERMONT
(with Margaret Hard)

Walter Hard's
VERMONT PEOPLE

Edited by
Walter Hard, Jr.
J. Kevin Graffagnino

1981
VERMONT BOOKS
Middlebury

ISBN 0-911570-18-7

Library Of Congress # 81-51414

Most of these poems have appeared in the *Manchester
Journal*, and in the *Rutland Herald*. To these Vermont
newspapers, grateful acknowledgement is made.

Printed in Vermont, U.S.A.

EDITORS' NOTE

This volume is a selection of Walter Hard's poems which have not previously appeared in book form. Chosen from newspaper clippings which form part of the Walter Hard Papers collection in the University of Vermont's Bailey/ Howe Library, they are a harvest of forty years of Hard's writing.

Original punctuations and spellings have been followed in general.

The reader would do well to keep in mind Dorothy Canfield Fisher's *caveat* that the poems "lose their flavor if read too many at one sitting." Absorb them a few at a time, with some thought about the situations and the people and you'll enjoy them more deeply.

WALTER HARD, JR.
J. KEVIN GRAFFAGNINO

INTRODUCTION

"If Walter Hard doesn't qualify as poet laureate of Vermont he certainly is to be considered as a serious runner-up, and he is young enough so that there is a lot of running, probably, left in him." It was July, 1931, and columnist Charles E. Crane of the *Brattleboro Daily Reformer* had just finished reading a slim volume of verse entitled *Salt of Vermont*. The object of Crane's admiration was an unassuming, forty-nine year old drugstore owner from Manchester whose work was little-known outside southwestern Vermont. Crane was not alone then in his estimation of Walter Hard's writing, and in the thirty-five years that followed an ever-widening circle of both critics and general readers came to appreciate his literary talents. By the time he died in 1966 at the age of eighty-four, Walter Hard had published nine volumes of poetry and two of prose about the Green Mountain State and fully earned the unofficial title of Poet Laureate. For thousands of natives, newcomers and expatriates alike, he was the leading voice of Vermont.

Possibly no author has taken more to heart the old maxim of "write about what you know best" than Walter Hard. The fifth generation of his family to live in the Battenkill Valley, he absorbed all the folklore, traditions, stories, anecdotes and tall tales that his Yankee forebears and their neighbors had passed down over the years. Three decades as reluctant proprietor of the family drugstore kept Hard from realizing his youthful dream of a career as a country newspaper editor, but they added many a face and many an incident to the raw material from which he would distill the "mountain township" of his poems. Whatever his profession or avocation at different periods in his long life—merchant, civic leader, bookseller, state legislator, author—"Vermonter" was the term that described Hard best, and it was invariably about Vermont that he wrote.

Walter Hard was past forty before he even embarked on his literary career. In the 1920's he began to write a whimsical editorial column for the *Manchester Journal* and the *Rutland Herald*, closing each offering with a selection from his rich stock of local stories. The stories seemed a bit stiff in prose on the printed page, so he soon devised a homemade form of verse for telling them. The poems proved very popular with readers of the two papers, and for the next four decades he devoted Sundays after church to writing his weekly column. Hard greatly enjoyed the role of part-time newspaperman, and, with a little notebook always at hand for recording new bits of Yankee wit and wisdom, he never ran low on ideas for his Vermont verse.

When he collected a sampling of his newspaper poems for publication in book form, Hard soon found that his work carried a good deal of appeal outside Vermont. His wry humor and pithy descriptions of life in rural Yankeedom touched sympathetic chords all over America. "Poetry for the man who does not like poetry," his books brought him loyal fans from Maine to Oregon. Nine volumes of verse, from *Some Vermonters* (1928) through *Vermont Sampler* (1963), offered readers what *Life* magazine called "anecdotes, with the flavor of stories lovingly told by deliberate countrymen around a red-hot stove," and Hard became one of the most popular regional poets of his generation.

Unlike most popular poets, Hard was also a great success with serious literary critics. Metropolitan reviewers worried about the precise definition of his unconventional verse forms, but agreed that they were "something new in American literature—something genuine and firsthand . . . as solid and real as blocks of Dorset marble." Colleges such as Harvard, Wesleyan, Cornell and Dartmouth offered speaking engagements or included Hard's books in their required reading lists for American literature classes; scholarly treatises on regional folklore made much of his Yankee stories; and Hard's alma mater, Williams College, awarded him an honorary degree in 1933. On an individual basis, his list of eminent fans included Carl Sandburg ("I treasure and reread his volumes."), Alexander Woollcott, Louis Untermeyer, Carl Carmer, Robert Frost and many others who placed Hard's poetry "in the gallery of the best that has been done by the regionalists of the earth."

The world of Walter Hard's poems was the Manchester area where his ancestors had lived and died, and where he spent his entire life. He faithfully detailed the scenes and inhabitants of the small country town, "a matter of fifty houses." His characters—George Stone, Ed Brayley, Josiah Scroby, Old Rob, Eliza Parkinson, Sam Perron and all the rest—called to mind the real-life individuals after whom he had modeled them. The balance of his portraits, as well as the liberal sprinkling of dry humor, made Hard's creation a generally likeable and wholly believable community. A Vermont version of "Edgar Lee Masters, without the sting and bite," according to Sinclair Lewis, Hard painted a unique picture of life in a rural Yankee environment.

Yet Hard's village transcended representation of a single New England town. His poems presented Manchester as a microcosm, a tiny lens through which to view the common condition. With lives that encompassed much of the breadth of human existence, Hard's characters became more than just quaint Vermont originals; their feelings, prejudices, joys, sorrows and philosophies demonstrated basic responses to the variety of life's experiences. As he wrote in "The Village," Hard's Manchester was universally human in scope:

> A sleepy village in a peaceful valley.
> Yet, friend, there life stages its drama.
> Tragedy, comedy, nobility beside self-seeking:
> Petty crimes against the spirit;
> The wise serenity of old age;
> The rebellious passion of youth.
> There the whole of life unfolds
> From childhood's carefree days
> To that hillside with the white stones.
> Fifty houses offering the life of the race.

In Hard's poems the key to the life available in his "sleepy village" lay in Vermont's retention of long-established traditions. Hard perceived this rural society as slipping away across much of America, and he consciously stressed the simple lifestyle and time-honored values that earlier generations had bequeathed to him and his neighbors. He found tremendous dignity in this quiet, unpretentious existence. His poems praised those—Captain Dever, Martha Powell, Zadock Haywood, Eben Sedgwick, Ellen Twitchell—who gave something of themselves to their community and "were big enough not to amount to much." Others might have drawn his characters as backward country bumpkins, but to Hard the lives of the hardworking Yankees around him carried their own nobility.

Not surprisingly, the Vermont landscape and natural environment exerted a great deal of influence on Hard's characters. They joked about the rocky soil and the long winters, but for the most part (like Henry Stoddard in "Green Vs. White"), his neighbors drew strength and sustenance from their surroundings:

Henry used to sit on the porch after supper
And watch the twilight settle on the waiting valley.
He watched winter storms sweep along the
    mountain tops
And then drift down to blot out the valley.
Somehow, the sight of those mountains and that
    reaching valley
Brought peace to Henry's soul.
Or the strength of its storms stirred an
    answering something
In his blood.
Not that he thought it all out.
He took it into his being as he did breath into
    his lungs.

As Hard's poems showed, this combination of the scenic and the untamed qualities of Nature added something very special to life in the "mountain township."

For Walter Hard, as for others of his generation, the outside pressures that threatened their rural Vermont were cause for some alarm. While the newcomers and tourists in his poems were more amusing than truly worrisome, Hard found many of the larger, impersonal forces of the twentieth century less benign. Surrounded by a nation growing sadly out of touch with the small-town traditions on which it was built, Hard's Vermont was not immune to the effects of progress. As early as the 1920's, and increasingly thereafter, much of Hard's incentive for writing about his chosen characters and themes came from a desire to show rural New England as it had been—and as he hoped part of it would always re-main.

Yet Hard's poems were not merely a collection of nostalgia for an irretrievable yesterday. Despite time and technology, Vermont to him remained better off than the rest of the country in the ways that really mattered. His neighbors had retained enough of their heritage so that the Green Mountain State still was, as he wrote in 1946 for the introductory issue of *Vermont Life*, a relative oasis of "stability and security, come what may." In Vermont the basic elements of early America— hard work, closeness to the land and an understanding of Nature, a simpler style of life, a sense of the past—continued to hold true. Hard's writings presented this view of Vermont for nearly forty years—at a time when the state's image was evolving nationally—and a widespread audience acquired lasting impressions of Vermont from his poems.

Influential with his own generation and that of his children, Hard's poetry remains equally relevant and timely today. The rural tradition lives on in Vermont, and Hard's verse still captures the essence of the people and the villages of his native state. In a broader context, his sharp character sketches continue to reflect his remarkable understanding of "the noble, the absurd, the pathetic and the triumphant in all human life." Formulated in the Jazz Age and repeated with slight variation into the Space Age, Walter Hard's philosophy has lost none of its richness as an articulate statement of the traditional small-town way of life.

Individuals who have read and enjoyed Walter Hard's poems in the past will find themselves on familiar ground with this new volume. Here are faithfully-rendered details of life in rural New England, from the local Fireman's Muster in "Fire Extinguishers" to Eben Wilder's cluttered shop in "Solo Work." Residents of the region will find many an everyday scene here, and probably an equal number of accurately-drawn Yankee personalities; there are few New England towns which lack their own versions of Ezra Stevens, Wallace Andrews, Miss Allenby or at least some cross-section of the other characters included in this collection. Finally, there is of course considerable Green Mountain humor here, a humor that highlights rather than obscures Hard's quiet insistence that there is something exceptional and admirable about his Vermonters.

As many have discovered, it is not necessary to be a Vermonter to relish Hard's poetry, although it will not hurt. Geography is not the determining factor in the potential for appreciation of his work. As his fellow regionalist Robert P. Tristam Coffin of Maine wrote, Walter Hard's poems "make good reading in any state."

J. Kevin Graffagnino
Curator, Wilbur Collection of Vermontiana
University of Vermont Library

Shelburne, Vermont
January, 1981

Old Friends

There had always been hard feeling
Between the Barker and the Smutts families.
Nobody seemed to know just how it began
But it was rumored that Old Man Barker
Beat Old Man Smutts in a cow trade
And Smutts evened up on a law suit
Over a piece of mountain land.
The sons' wives in each family
Kept the ill feeling going
Even when the sons were ready
To forgive and forget.
Then the Barkers moved away
And everybody forgot the row.

It was ten years later
When the "young" Barkers,
Now with a family of growing children,
Came back to the valley
For a visit.
They picked the time of the Fair
So they'd be sure to meet all the folks.
They were in front of Floral Hall
Holding quite a reception
When young Mrs. Smutts came along.
There was a general lull in the conversation.
A few suddenly remembered the old row.
Mrs. Smutts advanced and with elaborate politeness
Shook hands with Mrs. Barker.
She held her hand and then said sadly:
"My gracious, how you hev aged, Sary Barker."
Mrs. Barker blinked and withdrew her hand.
She looked Mrs. Smutts over from head to heel.
Then she said, with a toss of her head:
"Well, my lands,
I don't believe I shud ever knowed YOU
Ef it hedn't a' ben fer that dress."

Mine Host

Jim was not a born hotel keeper.
He had been born on a farm
Over the Mountain.
When he was old enough he took the farm over
And probably he'd have lived there all his days,
As his father and grandfather had done,
If his wife hadn't inherited the hotel
In the village over the Mountain.

Jim managed to keep up some of his farm work
Even as a hotelman.
He kept his two choice cows
And of course his driving horse.
He had several acres of land out back
Where he could raise about all
He wanted to cultivate.
His wife did the cooking
And looked after things in general
Including Jim.
Jim was apt to speak his mind
Even if he did insult a guest.
His wife had to smooth over many rough spots
Jim managed to rake up.
They were getting ready for Sunday dinner
And Jim, in his shirt sleeves,
Was freezing the ice cream in the shed.
His wife called to him that there was somebody
Stamping around in the office.
Her hands were in the dough.

Jim hurried in to find a stranger waiting.
Without stopping to answer Jim's curt "H'ware ye?"
He asked: "What yu chargin' fer dinner?"
"Seventy-five cents" Jim said wiping his brow.
"Seventy-five cents!" the stranger stared.
"That's pretty steep. I got seven in m' party."
Jim turned toward the kitchen door.
"Could a left some of 'em to home
Couldn't yu?" he said looking back at the stranger.

Neighborliness

Through the spring and early summer
Sidney Carford had been housed.
For a few weeks he had been confined to his bed
And even the Doctor had confessed
That he didn't "just like the look of things."
However, Sid's robust constitution and fighting spirit
Got him so he could sit out on his porch
When the warm days of July came.
Sid had always been a belligerent citizen
And he had been engaged in several law suits.
His row with Joe Simmons, who lived up the road a piece,
Never got as far as the courts.
However it divided the two families
So they were not on speaking terms.
It was all over dog and chicken trouble,
Sidney owning the chickens
And Joe owning the chasing dog.
The row had gone on for several years
Even though the dog had become too old
To make any attempt at violent exercise.
One day in late July Sidney was sitting in a rocker
On his front porch where he could see what was passing
He was better but his cheeks were still hollow
And he had to have a shawl over his legs.
He was beginning to assert himself again
And his wife had considerable trouble
Making him do as the doctor said he must.
Joe Simmons had usually avoided passing the house on foot
When he knew Sidney was likely to be out.
This day, one of Vermont's best,
He decided to walk to the village.
Moved by the beauty of everything around him
He decided to speak to Sidney if he was on the porch.
He wanted to be in tune with the universe.
So when he got to Sidney's house
And saw Sidney was sitting out in the sun
He stopped and called out from the sidewalk:
"Well, Sidney, how're you feelin' this mornin'?"
He took a step toward the porch.
Sidney pulled the shawl closer around his knees.
He looked at Joe from under his bushy eyebrows.

3

"It's none of your damned business how I am," he said.
And then he added in a lower tone:
"And I wouldn't tell you that much
If you wa'nt a neighbor."

Plumb Foolish

Shel had two reputations to support.
One was his standing as one of the best stone masons
That ever operated in the valley.
The other was his ability to hold more red liquor,
And still navigate, than any person in the County.
There were those that even extended the latter superiority
To cover the state or even beyond its bounds.
His reputation had been enhanced on both counts
By the often repeated story of his Sunday emergency job
On the plugged cesspool of a summer resident minister.
He had reported that Shel had not only done a good job
But that he had found him singing gospel hymns
While he worked in the unpleasant surroundings
That of necessity obtained.
The minister even used Shel as an example of Christian virtue
When he was later back in his city pulpit.
For obvious reasons he had not been able
To get a whiff of Shel's breath.
Partly as a result of the minister's praises
Shel was hired by another summer visitor
Who was remodelling an old house he'd bought.
One of the first considerations had been the chimney.
The new owner had Shel over to look it over.
Shel had at once decided that it should be laid over
But the owner wasn't sure it really needed it.
To prove his point Shel went up on the roof
And set old man Howard, who was working around the place,
To watch below when he let the plumb line down.
"How is she?" Shel called from the roof.
"She's all right" the old man yelled back.
"Is she plumb?"
"Lord, yes," the old man shouted.
"She's plumb and two inches t' spare."

4

Brother Against Brother

George and Frank were brothers.
They never got along together.
They fought all through childhood
And when they were men grown
They often came to blows.
George was a hard worker and thrifty.
Frank was shiftless and always poor.
Now and then Frank would get in a bad mess
And George would help him out
Just for the sake of the family.

It was to help him save his farm
That George loaned Frank
Five hundred dollars
And took his note for it.
It ran along for some years,
And each time George tried
To get something out of Frank
There was some tale of hard luck.
He'd lost a cow or a horse
Or his corn crop had failed.
Then George discovered one day
That he'd lost the note.
He hunted high and low
But he couldn't find it.

At last, after it was outlawed,
He found it in the butt'ry
Between two plates,
Up on the top shelf.
He'd just had an awful row with Frank
And he took the papers to a lawyer
To see if he couldn't force payment.
The lawyer shook his head
When he looked at the date.
George argued and plead.
Finally the lawyer said, there was only one way
He could collect.
If it could be proved that when he
Had made the loan he was *non compos mentis*
Then something might be done about it.

"Wal b'gol" George said, getting up from his chair,
"Don't that there paper
Prove I was er I wouldn't never
Hev took it, would I?"

Tom Comes To Life

There was nothing in the family records
Which would tell how old Tom was.
He had been adopted by the family
Some years before when the women folks
Demanded a driving horse of their own.
All of George Elkin's horses were high steppers
And not the kind for those who wished to jog along
With safety, and not speed, as their chief demand.
Tom was certainly safe.
George said you had to squint across the fence
To tell which way he was going.
Mrs. Elkins used him when she went to town
And on Sunday she always drove him to meeting.
Judging by his teeth Tom was past thirty,
And judging by his speed he was past fifty.
Naturally George Elkins had no use for him.

* * *

One morning in autumn George went to the barn.
He fed his real horses first,
Looking each of them over
With a loving eye.
When he went to throw some grain
Into the manger of old Tom
He found him stretched out stiff and cold.
Later in the morning he put him on a stone boat
And carried him to the upper pasture.
George thought when he had time he'd bury him.
That night when he went for the cows
To his consternation there stood old Tom,
His head over the bars, whinnying for supper.
The hot sun of the fall day
Had started the blood coursing again.
George was telling about it.
"The darned old fool. He never did know nothin'.
He didn't even know enough
T' know when he was dead."

Firing Squad

Usually Mr. Tumpkins was a mild mannered man.
Sometimes his sermons contained thunderbolts
But they were generally hurled at sinful generalities.
He was not what you'd call a meek man exactly—
He had the cockiness which often goes with small stature.
Folks who knew him, as all the village did,
Knew this was all on the surface.
It was really all that was left of his early days.
Mrs. Tumpkins had married her minister husband
And entered upon her duties with missionary zeal.
He had become one of her first converts—or victims.
Physically she was superior in size and strength.
Gradually she chipped off the corner of his personality.
By the time they had settled in the village
He was shaped to suit her desires.
When he was out alone sometimes he emerged.
That occurred so seldom that few people ever really knew him.
When the prohibition question was up for a vote
He suddenly took on new life.
He preached fiery sermons showing an amount of zeal
Which nobody suspected he had.
In private conversation afterward he was as calm as usual.
In fact he didn't seem too much interested in prohibition
Except for his fiery pulpit utterances.
Deacon Cornhill was talking about it in his store one day.
He had been somewhat worried by the minister's public zeal
And his failure to carry on outside of the pulpit.
Thomas Older, the other deacon, listened to Deacon Cornhill
Without saying anything.
"I jest can't make it out," Deacon Cornhill went on.
"I never heard him pitch in as he has been these last sabbaths
Then's soon's he's outside he hasn't a word t' say."
Deacon Older looked at the floor and smiled.
"I guess mebbe I kin understand," he said.
"Ma Tumpkins loads the gun;
Pa fires it."

Out Of Court

A group of men
Was gathered under a maple
In front of the Court House.
Some were in their shirt sleeves,
Their coats of Sunday black
Carefully laid on the ground.
From the window of the court room
Came the voice of a lawyer
Passionately addressing the jury.
Now just a quiet beseeching,
Gradually working up into a shout.
The group under the tree
Paid no attention to the lawyer's voice.
They were listening to a tall man
Who leaned against the maple tree
His narrow brimmed straw hat
Tipped back on his head.
He was discussing a case
Which had just been finished.
Some of the men in the group
Had been witnesses.
"Well sir, I sez t' him,"
The tall man was continuing.
"If I ever come home
And ketched a strange man
Akissin' my woman"—
He squared his shoulders.
"I'd throw him out th' winder
No matter how hard 'twas rainin'."

No Information

Where the car crossed the mountain
The signs of spring were just beginning to show.
The leaf buds on the bushes
Were still tight-rolled cones,
Except where the sun had tempted a few
To show a little more of their new green.
The dead leaves in the woods were still pressed flat.
Only here and there new growth,

8

Driven by the urgency of spring,
Had lifted up the cover to get the sun.
As the valley began to open below them
The men in the car noticed the spreading green.
There were leaves large enough
To cast shadows on the road
And along the streams and on the lately cut slopes
Here and there a shad bush in full bloom stood out.
As they went past marshy places
The frogs were jangling their sleigh-bells.
The car stopped at a crossroad
Where there was a sign post but no sign.
After some discussion they turned off the main road
Onto a narrow winding one which soon showed little use.
Coming around one of the frequent bends
They saw a man evidently preparing to fish.
They drew alongside and asked him,
"Can you tell us, is this the road to Averill?"
The fisherman was tall and thin with a drooping look.
As though he'd been startled out of a dream
He looked up the road and then back at the men.
"Wal now, I can't tell ye.
Don't rightly know m' self."
As the men started the car again
They noticed another fisherman in the stream.
Driving carefully in low gear they moved off.
They'd gone only a short distance on the rutty road
When they heard the man they'd been talking to, shouting.
They stopped and saw him hurrying down the road.
They started backing, keeping to the track with difficulty.
Out of breath he came up to the car.
"I jest wanted t' tell ye," he said, halting between words,
"I asked m' friend back there
And he don't know whether this rud
Goes t' Averill, either."

Seeing Snakes

Ed Wilson had been out West.
Of course a lot of folks had gone
But Ed was one of the first to come back.
He only stayed about a year.

He just came back on business.
Nobody who had ever been in the wide open spaces
Would ever settle down in the East again.
So he was going to leave at any moment
For years—until he got too feeble
To think any more about the West.

He was full of tales
About his adventures
On the plains and in the mountains.
He viewed the ranges which surrounded the valley
With utter contempt.
They were just hills compared to what he'd seen.

At the cider mill one day,
He was telling of a close call he'd had
When he was riding along a narrow trail.
A rattler had struck his horse
And he had just saved himself
From going over the cliff.
Old man Stockwell sat on a bag of apples.
When Ed had finished his story,
The old man scratched his head.
Putting his hat back he said:
"Never heered 'bout my fightin' a snake, did yu?"
He took a bite from a greening he found in the bag.
"I was hoein' pertaters up on th' Slocum place.
I'd put a jug o' water in the bushes out th' sun.
I'd jest finished drinkin' when I heered a rustlin'.
Afore I knowed what was happnin' a snake whizzed past me."
He chewed on his apple for a minute.
"I took after 'im with m' hoe.
I cornered him and he coiled.
Wal sir he struck afore I did and missed me!
But he hit that hoe handle square."
The old man got up and picked up the bag of apples.
"It wan't five minutes afore that hoe handle
Had swelled up twice as big ez yer arm."

Dog Tired

Wallace Andrews farmed it alone.
It was not a one-man farm
But he managed to get along
By leaving many things undone.
He usually started a new job
With a great show of work
But he finished only a part of it.
He was apt to mow
More than he could get in.

Wallace had mowed for two days
In the meadow south of the house.
They had been perfect hay days.
By the time he got the hay raked up
It had grown sultry
And thunder caps had gathered.
Along in the afternoon
He'd drawn in two loads
When dark clouds appeared over Equinox
And thunder muttered in the distance.

Instead of hustling
As all his neighbors were doing
To get in all he could before the rain
He started for the barn
With less than half a load.
He drove through the gate onto the road
His old dog following behind
With his dripping tongue
Nearly dragging on the ground.

Cephas Eliot drove past.
He drew up for a minute.
"Wal I vum, Wallace," he said
"What's the matter of ye
Bringin' in a little jag like that
And aleavin' all that hay t' git wet.
'Twon't rain fer half an hour yit."

Wallace leaned on his fork.
He looked at the dog

And said quietly, as if he didn't want
Shep to hear:
"Wal, y' see I thought th' dog
Seemed t' be gittin' a leetle tired."

Absent Minded

On Friday morning there was always extra activity
Around the Buxton farmhouse.
That was the day Alfred and his wife went to town
Carrying their butter and eggs and perhaps some vegetables.
They'd come back around five with the wagon-box
Well filled with all the things their large family demanded.
Almeda spent her time with her sister
While Alfred took care of the day's business.
Alfred was large, good natured and very forgetful.
The older children often made fun of his absentmindedness
And he usually joined in.
Almeda wasn't endowed with much sense of humor
And she viewed her husband's failures to remember
As something to be borne—but not in silence.
She was systematic and methodical in all her work
And she tried in vain to train the children in her ways.
So the good times the family had together often left Almeda out.
One Friday Almeda had handed Alfred an unusually long list
When they started out from the house.
And she recalled to his mind that there had been times
When even with her carefully prepared lists
He'd come home with important things missing.
Alfred started home around three that afternoon.
He'd got rid of all his produce and he'd done all his errands.
He was smiling over a story the miller had told him
As he drove out of the village and along the river.
Gradually a feeling that he had forgotten something
Crept into his mind.
Unable to get rid of it he finally pulled Almeda's list
Out of his pocket and spread it on his knee.
He couldn't think of a thing he'd missed
So he put it back and settled down in the seat.
As the horses began the long steady climb into the hills
He hummed a little tune over and over
Matching the tone with the crickets' fiddling.
As he got nearer home the feeling that he'd forgotten something

Began to annoy him again.
He stopped the team and taking his list he checked
    over the bundles
Which were in boxes back of him and on the seat beside him.
Finding everything there he clucked to the horses.
As he drove into the yard the three younger children,
Just home from school, hurried down the home lane to meet him.
As he drew near they stopped and looked.
Suddenly they were silent.
Then in a subdued chorus they asked:
"Where's Ma?"

Bondville Fair

The Bondville Fair never had a smooth track,
Nor any horse racing at all.
For years no steam calliope sent its shrill tones
Echoing along the close-by wooded hills.
No crowded grandstand cheered gay vaudevillians
And no Ferris Wheel rolled squealing riders
Up above the tree-tops.
It was mostly a home-made thing to begin with
As Fairs in general were.
Only since the automobile has made Bondville nearby
Has the Fair taken on some of the habiliments
Of its much more sophisticated neighbors.
Holly Johnson went to the first Bondville Fair.
For the first few years it was held in the street
With small displays and only one or two contests.
That was sixty-three years ago.
There was some diluted lemonade
And on the side considerable undiluted cider.
It wasn't the current vintage, generally, either.
The management or at least many of the attendants
Have always followed the reasoning of a fellow townsman
Who was preparing to go to Brattleboro to the circus.
He said he always advised taking several good drinks
Of any potent beverages obtainable before attending a circus.
"It allays makes them wild animals look so much larger."
After the street had been used for a few years
Holly says they moved up on the hill
Back of what was then Stiles' hotel.

"No," he said, "there wasn't a level spot
Bigger 'n your bandannah up there but they made out."
Holly's blue eyes turned toward the past
And he smiled and then went on.
"Along aftah dinnah they'd begin rollin' down th' hill.
More and more of 'em toppled ovah and rolled down
And when they was all cawded up to the bottom
The Faiah was ovah."

Fair Warning

It was a night
With cold glittering stars.
The snow crunched under the feet
Of the few people who were abroad.
They walked with hunched shoulders
And their heads drawn into their coat collars.
Inside the depot the group of loafers
Was reduced to three.
They were waiting for the evening train to pull in.
It was already half an hour late
And they were speculating as to the cause.

Mert Sanderson had little to say.
He sat bent forward in his chair.
From time to time he'd hold his palms
Up to the stove.
He kept his hat drawn over his ears
And his feet as close to the stove as was safe.

The station agent went out for a minute
Leaving the door open.
He was a new man on the job
And this thoughtlessness
Didn't add to his popularity.
He came in stamping his feet
And went into the ticket office
Where a telegraph was ticking busily.

Finally Mert decided it was time
That something was said.
"Raymond," he called toward the ticket window,

"You'd better come out
And stir up this fire here."
After a time Raymond came out.
He shook the fire vigorously
And then emptied a hod of coal on it.
"You want t' keep things comf'able here, Raymond,"
Mert said rubbing his hands,
"'Cause if you don't
We'll just move up t' the hardware store
T' do our loafin'."

Past Glory

"Whay Boss! Whay there!"
Henry was driving his cows
From the pasture at the foot of the mountain
Up the village street.
A little stooped,
His joints stiffened with rheumatism
He shuffled along behind his cows
Brandishing a maple stick
When one stopped for an extra nibble of grass.
The stick was worn smooth and shiny
With its daily trips to and from the pasture.
About all people ever heard Henry say
Was "Whay boss! Whay!"
He was an old man who drove cows.

* * *

When the stage road across to Brattleboro
Ran from Bennington through Wilmington
It was Henry who made the route famous.
Young, erect, proud of his calling
He used to roll into Wilmington
Cracking his long whip
Over the foam flecked leaders.
At dusk he would rattle into Brattleboro
And pull up at the Tavern with a flourish.
As he stepped down from the box
His long whip in his hand,
And greeted the hostlers familiarly.
The boys stood around

Wrapped in admiration.
Then and there many a boy picked his career.

* * *

Now as he shuffled through the dust
Driving his cows home in the twilight
A small boy stuck his head from behind a tree
And called: "Whay boss! Whay there!"
And ducked back out of sight.

Jake Speaks

Jake Weston had an ornery disposition.
Whether it was a matter of inheritance,
Early environment, or liver,
Nobody seemed to be sure.
In fact there was little speculation as to the cause.
He was a good blacksmith, a hard worker,
And as such he was respected.
Only a few ever tried to argue with him.
When anyone did he was usually silenced
By the decisive finality of Jake's utterances.
Probably his profession saved him considerable trouble.
He could take it out on a piece of hot iron
And at the same time be doing useful work.
Folks wondered how his wife ever put up with him.
She knew him.

Jake was especially scornful of public men.
The more they were praised
The more he found fault with them.
If he ever had a good word
It was for the under dog.

Perhaps others felt as he did about the Squire,
But he was the only one who openly attacked him.
He always called him "Old Eight Per Cent."
The Squire was really the biggest man in the town.
He was an office holder of ability
And he was sometimes very charitable.
He was still Old Eight Per Cent to Jake.

The Squire had been sick all summer.
He was well over seventy and when he got out again

He showed his age for the first time.
He went past Jake's shop one afternoon.
Jake was shoeing a horse for John Fielding.
John said: "Well, the Squire ain't the man he ust t' be."
Jake rasped the hoof on his knee.
"No," he said, "and he never was."

Wages

When Hiram Turner left home
He had to walk all the way to Bennington
Because nobody happened
To be driving that way.
Any cash outlay was not thought of
Because he had less than a dollar.

He wasn't much of a hand to write,
So it was ten or more years
Before folks heard about him.
Then somebody came back from the West
And said they'd seen Hiram
And he seemed quite prosperous.

Gradually as time went on
Word came that Hiram Turner
Was head of a big concern
Some where beyond Chicago.
It was the summer after that
That he suddenly appeared in the village.
He looked up all the "boys"
And seemed glad to see them.
Maria Swett said he seemed
"Jest as natural like
And not one mite stuck up."

He met 'Lish Towne at the grist mill.
'Lish helped there sometimes.
He'd never more than made ends meet
And he was always ready to try something new.
After talking over old days
He took Hiram to one side.
And asked him for a job.
Hiram thought a minute

And then told him he could give him work
In one of his own plants.
'Lish got all the details.
Finally, all ready to go, he said:
"What wages do ye pay, Hiram?"
"Well, you come out with me
And try it. We'll pay you what you're worth."
"Gosh, Hiram, I can't afford
T' work fer no sech wages as that."

The Office Seeks The Man

For many years Silas Bent
Had been Selectman.
As he got older he got more sot
And the voters found fault with him.
When he came up for re-election
There would be talk of running this one or that
But each time Silas was chosen.
They didn't want to hurt the old man's feelings.

The first Town Meeting after Silas died
There were all sorts of rumors afloat.
At least a dozen men were said to be running—
Most of them unfitted for the office.
Finally a few of the more careful ones
Got together and talked the matter over.
They decided to sound out Elijah Strong.
He had never held office.
He had never taken any active part in the town.
But he was a good farmer
And they thought if he could run his own business
He might be trusted to help run the town's.
Sid Stockwell was delegated to interview 'Lijah.
He found his man getting ready to milk.
He stood around while 'Lijah was milking the first cow.
He talked about things in general
And finally edged toward the matter in hand.

Three cows had been milked
Before Sid got a final answer.
He had used all of his arguments
And 'Lijah had put him off with generalities.

Finally he got up from the third cow
And stood with the milking stool in one hand.
"No sir. I tell yu I ain't runnin' fer no office.
I've allus been a damned old son-of-a-gun
But there ain't only a few that knows it.
Ef I was t' run fer office
Ev'rybody in th' county'd know it,
And I jest ain't agoin' t' run, that's all."

Solo Work

If anybody in the valley
Wanted a neat bit of work done in wood
They always went to the small shop back of Brayley's.
It really wasn't so small
But it was so cluttered up that it seemed so.
The windows were covered with sawdust and cobwebs
Of many years gathering.
Shavings and sawdust were everywhere inside too,
And each year they filled more space.
In spite of this Eben Wilder worked away at his bench
And whatever he turned out was well done.
Hanging from nails and from the rafters
There were chairs with carved backs,
And a bundle of table legs all hand done.
And all sorts of odd pieces made for someone
Who never came after them.
Eben wouldn't sell a thing from the lot
Because the one who ordered it might turn up.
Eben himself was broad shouldered and heavy
But his shoulders were stooped with so much standing.
His face was round and his cheeks stuck out
Like a chipmunk's when he's been foraging.
A sandy moustache made his face look cluttered
And his thick glasses added to the effect.
He was always either humming a tune
Or, if he was very intent on his work,
He'd talk to himself.
One time one of the boys in the village
Had listened for some time to Eben's one-sided conversation.
Eben was so intent on his work he didn't know the boy was there
And the boy was so amazed at what he heard
He stood for quite a while in awed silence.

Finally Eben saw him and changed to humming a tune.
The boy stood around a while and then took courage to ask:
"Why were you talking to yourself, Mr. Wilder?"
Eben straightened up and squinted along a board
   he was planing.
"Well, young man," he said,
"First off I like to talk to an intelligent listener."
He put the board back in the vice and tightened it up.
"Besides, I like to listen t' someone that's got suthin' t' say."

Blind Love

A cloud of tobacco smoke
Made dimmer the feeble lights
In Brayley's store.
There was an unusually large congregation
Sitting around the chunk stove.
Even the counters were occupied.
It was Thanksgiving eve
And they all wanted to talk over the turkey shoot
Which had been held back of the village
That afternoon.

When a persistent customer got the attention
Of Brayley, he reluctantly took up a hand lamp
And went to the front.
Brayley tried no high pressure salesmanship.
He got the sale over as soon as possible
And hurried back to the stove.

He'd been detained to the point of exasperation
By Ella Burbank who wanted to match a piece of cloth.
When he regained his chair
Somebody was telling about Alfred Stokes getting married.
Alfred had lived alone ever since his mother died.
He never seemed to take any interest in women
And folks considered him a confirmed bachelor.

Brayley was as much surprised as anybody.
It seemed that Alfred had gone away the day before.
He'd come back that afternoon with a wife.
Luke Sykes the stage-driver took them to the house.
He gave some details about the trunk she brought

And how Alfred looked sheepish carrying a bird cage.
"Must a be'n a case of love at first sight,"
Somebody said.
The stage-driver snorted:
"Wal, I got a good look at 'er
And I reckon it must 'a' be'n."
He stretched and yawned.
"If he'd 'a' took a second look
He couldn't never 'a' done it."

Fire Extinguishers

There was a fire company in the village
And another at Factory Point.
Each company was named for its engine.
The one at the Point was the Pacific
And the other one was the Undine.
Of course they were pumped by hand
And there was plenty of rivalry
Between the two companies.

In those days a Firemans Muster
Was a real occasion.
Often a dozen or more companies
Would meet, with bands playing
And much marching, each company
Dressed in gay uniforms,
With their engines polished and glistening.
There were royal battles
To see which engine could throw the highest
And which one the farthest.
Pumping those long handles up and down
Took skill and endurance and team work.
Then the winner with its band
Headed a triumphal march through the town,
Through lines of shouting people.
The Pacifics were practising one afternoon
With the Undines in the street at the village.
They were shooting streams over the Liberty Pole
When Lampson came along.
He'd been sawing wood with his horse-power.
He stopped to watch.
One of the engines shot a stream
Straight up over the Pole.

Sam Peters turned to Lampson:
"How does that pumpin' hit ye, Lampson?"
Lampson picked up the reins.
"Hump, I'd put out a fire
With a cord o' green popple
Quicker'n both them engines could.
Giddap there."

Agricultural Economics

Steve was sitting on the narrow porch
Of his hostelry, his chair tipped back against the wall.
He carefully whittled the end of a match to a point
And proceeded to do some thorough excavating
In the oral cavity.
The peace of a summer afternoon
Rested on the village street.
The one horse in front of Cone & Burton's
Stamped a front foot, rested, and stamped the other.
A screen door slammed in the house next.
The clock in the church steeple struck two.

A buckboard crossed the bridge
And rattled down the road.
Steve woke with a start
That dropped his chair onto its four legs.
By the time he was fully awake
The buckboard drew up in front.
Baldwin wound the lines around the whip.
He lifted himself out and came toward Steve.
"Got another o' them hog's livers. Want it?"
Steve got up, stretched, and went toward the steps.
"If it's as good as that last one I can use it."
Baldwin went to the buckboard and brought out a basket.
From it he took the liver wrapped in newspaper.
"Leave it with Edna in the kitchen," Steve said.
"Stop in the office an' get yer pay."
Baldwin started toward the kitchen and then stopped.
"I'll hev t' git a cent more a pound fer this 'un," he said.
Steve turned quickly.
"A cent more? That's some rise in a week. How come?"
Baldwin looked belligerent.
"Wal by gosh, ain't I fed this critter a week longer?"

A Die-Hard

Of course Eph. Henderson
Was opposed to the coming of the Railroad.
He fought against the town's buying its bonds
And he had a lawsuit before he'd let the survey
Be made across the corner of his meadow.
It was a swampy corner a half mile from the house
But Eph. knew the new fangled Engine of the Devil
Would wreck his home sooner or later.

In spite of the few die-hards
The rails had been laid through the valley.
There were piles of wood in the shed
At the end of the new Depot.
Eph. had found that some of his supporters,
In his fight against the road,
Had suddenly deserted.
Later he found they were selling wood
To feed the new monsters which drew the cars.

The day the road opened most of the population
Assembled at the station to see the first train.
Eph. vowed he'd not go near the thing.
After his wife had gone
He sneaked over the hill and watched the smoke cloud
Come up along the straight stretch south of his meadow.
He stood fascinated in spite of himself
As the clattering train swept across the corner of his meadow.
It was going almost twelve miles an hour they said.
That evening Eph. sat by the kitchen stove.
As his wife told of the celebration at the Depot
Eph. sat opening and shutting his jack knife.
Now and then he grunted.
"Yes, Ephraim, I cal'late that Rail Rud
Is agoin' t' be awful convenient and I want to ride on it."
Eph. snapped the knife blade back.
He put the knife in his pocket and turned toward his wife.
"I see the tarnation thing a-spewin' smoke and sparks.
It come along head on up the valley and no harm done."
He stood up and shook his finger toward the meadow.
"But 'sposing it come up sidewise.
By mighty, it 'ud sweep everythin' afore it."

Anti-Freeze

That overflowing spring on the side of the hill
Above the house on the Simmons place
Was famous up and down the valley.
The three generations of Simmons who had lived on the farm
Realized it was one of their chief assets.
Sometimes they seemed to feel some credit was their due
For having such a spring on their place.
Youngsters, once they had been up to see it,
Used the fact with others not so fortunate
In boasting of their superiority.
To be truthful many were disappointed at first.
They'd expected a stream gushing from the side of the hill
But all they saw was a quiet pool
Just below the ledge of moss covered rock.
The constant bubbling didn't seem to amount to much
Until they saw the swift flowing outlet stream
Which never changed the depth of the feeding pool.
Willie Holler liked to watch that flow
As it glided out of sight down the hill
Especially in winter when ice covered twigs
Were constantly waving along the edges.
What he could not understand was why it never froze over.
No matter how much his father talked about
    the low thermometer
Water was always flowing freely from the ice-free pool.

One especially cold morning several men were standing
In front of Brayley's store where an ancient Ford
Was standing with steaming rusty water spreading under it.
It was Willie Holler who had become the proud owner
As soon as he was old enough to get a license.
Not that he was mechanically inclined.
He was not well enough equipped mentally.
He was just crazy over handling so much power.
He lifted up the hood. "That does beat all," he said.
"They told me t' put in kerisene or suthin' like,
When it got cold but gosh I didn't see no need.
I've watched that Simmons spring water
When it was way below zero and it don't never freeze.
I filled 'er up first sign o' freezin' weather
And here it's froze up and bursted first real cold day."

24

A Good Reason

Steve Allister cared more for horses
Than he ever did for any human being.
He came naturally by his passion
Since his father raised them on the farm,
And Steve grew up hearing horse talk
From the time he was old enough to know
What the word meant.
He sat in his father's lap and "drove"
As soon as he could hold the reins.
By the time he was in his teens
He was helping break colts to harness and saddle
And his specialty came to be the tough ones.
He had a way with them just as his father had.
When he began going with Bess Talbot,
Who was equipped with black hair
Snapping black eyes and a temper to match,
People decided he encountered the same challenge
He met and conquered in the wildest colts he tamed.
Several times during the period of courtship
They quarreled violently and for days
Were not on speaking terms.
Once a neighbor overheard their wild arguing
And she reported that their tongue lashing ability
Seemed to be about equal, with Bess having more staying power.
Then, quite suddenly, they were married by the Parson.
Perhaps, as the years passed,
Their arguing didn't mean as much deep down,
But Bess found frequent things to berate her husband about
And Steve refused to take her talk in silence.
One day Steve drove up the hill in front of his house.
He had a heavy load of stone on the wagon
And his well matched team of grays
Had to dig in and pull to get up the last steep pitch.
The Parson in his buggy waited by the gate
And Steve stopped his panting team across from him.
The Parson and Steve and Bess were long time friends.
"Steve," the Parson began, "How well that
    pair pulls together."
Steve admitted they were well matched.
"Might be a sermon there," the Parson continued looking
    off to the hills.

Steve smiled at his old friend.
"Well, you see, Parson, the thing is
That pair there 've got only one tongue between 'em."

Static

Jed Thomas wasn't what you'd call
A drinking man.
Probably if he had been
More regular in his drinking habits
The evidence of over-stimulation
Would not have been so conclusive.
As far as the records showed
Jed never drank at all
Except on the last day of the Fair.
On that day he did all his drinking for the year.
It only took a few good drinks of cider,
To produce the desired effect.

One year there had been so much trouble
With disturbances at the Fair
They had constables and sheriffs
From several towns around on the grounds.
Displaying bright badges they mixed with the crowds.

Along late in the afternoon
One of them came on Jed Thomas.
He was standing by the race track
Holding to the fence with both hands.
He seemed to be trying to catch something
Which was revolving rapidly,
But as soon as he let go of the fence
He immediately joined the rotating movement.

The constable approached Jed quietly
And touching him on the shoulder he said:
"Move along Jed, don't be standin' here."
With some difficulty Jed got his eyes focused
On the shining badge.
He spoke with an injured air:
"Moooove on, you shay.
Miser Sheruff, don' you shee
'Sall I c'n do
T' stay where I be?"

Band Night

It was band concert night.
Around the village green there were cars
Parked in double line.
In the center of the green, under bright lights,
The band, the pride of the village, sat.
Strings of colored lights stretched from the stand
To the trees at the three corners.
On the far side the Ladies' Aid served ice cream
And Cy Henderson dispensed pop-corn.
In and out among the crowd small boys
Chased each other, yelling as they ran.
When the band finished a piece
There was a long applauding blast
From the automobile horns.
The small boys were silenced for a moment.
From the pop-corn wagon came Cy's thin voice:
"Git yer pop-corn here. Jest popped and fresh buttered."
Some soldiers were camping on the Fair Grounds
And the cornet player of their band
Had been invited to play with the village band.
Silence fell even on the small boys
As the uniformed figure
Put his instrument to his lips.
The silver notes floated on the night air
Rising above the muted accompaniment.
He finished with a long run and then a final high clear note
That seemed to hang suspended above the tree tops
In the dark air before the stars began.
Harry turned to Nate who played a horn
In the village band.
"What 'd yu think of that?" he asked.
Nate took off his hat and scratched his head.
"Well," he said, "he didn't play that piece
JEST as I should 'a played it."

Spring In The Village

On the porch of Brayley's store
A brightly painted plow glistened in the sun.
The store door was open
And Brayley's old hound dozed on the door sill
Where he could keep track of things
Going on in the street and in the store.
A case of Budd D. Hawkins seeds
Stood near the post office boxes inside the door.
A rake and a spade and a hoe
Were leaned against the wall.
Across the road Mis' Benson's hens
Were enjoying a dust bath in the flower bed,
Their owner being at a meeting of the Sewing Circle.
In the vacant lot back of the school house
The children, out for the morning recess,
Were playing one old cat,
Exercising bodies and lungs at the same time.
When the bell rang they stopped reluctantly
And loitered by the door in the warming sun.
Then the only sound was the irregular putt putt
Of a gasoline engine and the zing of the saw
As it cut through the pieces of cord-wood.
Old Man Hazleton, sitting on the store steps,
Noticed how the engine slowed up on the bigger pieces
And then sailed along faster and faster
When the pressure let up.
He recalled the days when he used to saw wood by hand.
He could work up a cord a day then
And he didn't know what it meant to be tired.
No shirking work with any putt-putting engine.
He brought his cane down in protest against the times.
Just then a stranger drove up.
He got out and looked around, up and down the street.
Then he saw the old man sitting on the steps.
Hazleton had seen him coming toward him
But he didn't look up.
The man stopped in front of him.
"Nice spring day," he said.
"Makes out t' be," Hazleton replied still looking down.
The stranger found conversation hard going but he kept on.
Finally he remarked; "I suppose you've seen
    many changes hereabouts."

"Yes," he said, "I have."
He brought his cane down hard on the step.
"Been agin all of 'em too."

Education

Will Slocum had started
With nothing except a strong body
And a passion for work.
He gradually progressed from chore boy,
Working for his board and clothes,
To hired man with real wages.
He saved his wages
And when the Starkweather farm was for sale
He bought it with the help of a mortgage.
He married the girl who had worked on the farm
Where he began his career.
In five years he had paid up the mortgage
And from then on he prospered.

His first wife died.
In less than a year he married her sister.
Before he was fifty
He was a widower again.
But he was not inconsolable
And the following fall
He married the school teacher.
Folks were a little surprised
Because Will had never had any schooling.
He could write his name and that was all.
But he offered a comfortable home
And the school teacher was no longer young.

A few days after the wedding
Will came into Armstrong's store.
He passed the time of day with the storekeeper.
"Well, Will," Mr. Armstrong said
"How do you like you new wife?"
Will settled down in a chair by the stove.
"I don't see no diff'rance,
'Cept now 'stead o' sayin'
'Pass the taters' I say
Pass them PER taters."

Lost Or Found

About once a month during the summer
The scattered neighbors along the back hill road
Were sure to see Jed Beasley going toward town.
He had a good yoke of oxen and they were fast walkers
So the twelve mile trip down the valley,
While it demanded a fairly early start,
Left some time to Jed to do his trading
When he got to the big town.
It was Jed's custom to take along in his wagon
Whatever he had to sell or to trade for groceries.
He usually had a few orders for quarters of lamb
And he had regular customers for his butter.
In those days there were often several yoke of oxen
Standing with teams and single outfits in the big square
In the center of the business section of the town.
Jed usually tethered his oxen there and delivered his stuff
From a basket on foot.
When he was ready for home he'd stop in at the tavern.
He would take on board just enough liquor
So that when he got out on the road home
He'd be sleepy and curl up on the hay in the back of the wagon.
The oxen had always taken him home.
One afternoon he had been delayed and it was getting dark
By the time he got out onto the familiar road.
He had not omitted his potions
And, as usual, lay down on the hay and went promptly to sleep.
That night the oxen didn't stick to the road home.
They turned off to the left where there was an open barway.
The opening let them through but a wheel caught
And they got excited and lunged.
In a minute they were free of the wagon.
They took their own way out into the fresh green pasture.
Jed slept soundly until daybreak.
He sat up and gradually discovered what had happened.
Sitting there on the hay in the back of the wagon
He scanned the landscape and then took off his hat.
"Well," he said, addressing the atmosphere,
"If I'm Beasley I've lost me a good yoke o' oxen."
He took hold of the sides of the wagon and shook them.
"If I ain't Beasley I've found me
An allfired good wagon."

Legal Equipment

Zed Caldwell had come to the village
In response to a letter from Lawyer Jones.
The lawyer had won a damage suit for Zed
And he'd sent for him to come and get his money.
Zed had been on hand to testify.
He'd had to start home before the verdict came in
And the lawyer's letter was the first news he'd had
About the outcome of the case.

Zed walked into the lawyer's office
And seeing the stenographer
He wiped his hat from his head
And slicked his straggling locks with his hand.
"Well, I won your case, Mr. Caldwell."
Zed nodded. "I jedged so."
He handed Zed some bills.
"There's your money sir."
Zed counted slowly—Thirty-five dollars.
"How much d' je git?" he asked still eyeing the money.
"The jury awarded three hundred and sixty dollars.
I should say it was a very liberal award, Mr. Caldwell."
Zed counted the money again.
"That may seem a small amount for your share,
But you see, the sheriff's fees, writs and court costs
And then my fee, count up pretty fast.
But that's all yours. You're that much ahead."

Zed folded the bills until they made a tight wad.
He jammed the wad into his watch pocket.
With a glance at the stenographer, he took his hat,
And walked thoughtfully toward the door.
He put on his hat and opened the door.
Then he turned to the lawyer again.
"Don't want t' buy a hos, do ye?"
Lawyer Jones swung his chair around.
"Me, buy a horse? What would I want of a horse?"
Zed turned slowly, saying:
"Wal, Jesse James hed t' hev one."

Neighbors

The fact that the Perron farm
Was next to the Waller farm on the upper road
Naturally made the Perrons and the Wallers neighbors
But there were no neighborly feelings
Between the two families.
The bitter feeling went back a generation
As a result of some row over lines
And the sons carried it into the next generation.
There were times when there were signs
That they were going to at least sign a truce,
And then one or the other would neglect a fence
And the resulting trespassing of the cattle
Would start the whole thing up again.
Naturally the wives, getting the original story second-hand,
Were ready to end the struggle.
And the children of the two families
Going to the same district school
Forgot the family row most of the time.
There was even a time when the oldest Perron boy
Was sweet on the Waller daughter.
Then one day Sam Perron fell sick.
He gradually faded until, answering a question,
The doctor told him he was in mighty serious shape.
Pressed for the whole truth he told Sam
That if he had any business matters on his mind
It might be as well to call in his lawyer.
Sam had him sent for but first he insisted
He must see his neighbor Ed Waller.
Knowing the long enmity Sam's wife feared
That his mind might be failing
But the doctor said they'd better humor him anyhow.
Puzzled and somewhat suspicious Ed Waller
Entered the house for the first time in his life.
Sam held out a shrunken hand
As his wife raised him up on his pillow.
"Ed, we've fit all our lives and back of that
Our families started it." He spoke in a throaty voice
Stopping often for breath. "Now they say I'm likely
To be leavin'. I can't face m' maker . . .
With an enemy makin' a shadow . . ."
Ed took the hand, unable to speak a word.

Sam sank back on the pillow.
"There, I feel better," he whispered.
Fumbling for his handkerchief Ed made his way to the door.
From the bed came Sam's straining voice:
"Ed, I've tried . . to do . . right thing.
But Ed . . if I . . get well again . . ."
His voice was almost gone. "Y'understand . . .
This . . . . deal . . .'s all off."

Politics

Henry Stiles was fixing his fence
Which marked the highway
Along the valley road.
He didn't look up when a car
Clattered across the loose planks
Of the bridge over the brook.
When the tires slid on the gravel
Indicating to Henry a sudden stop
He turned around.
James Towers was turning the key in the switch.
He waved at Henry and said "H'war ye?"
In his usual genial manner.
"Mending fence?" he asked Henry as he drew near.
"Seems so," Henry said stamping on some loose dirt
Around the new set post.
James offered Henry a cigar
Which Henry took and put carefully in his pocket.
"Smoke it t' night," he said.
He looked at James with a half smile.
"You mendin' fence too?"
James was something of a power in local politics.
He'd been in the Legislature two terms
And now he was interesting himself
In the three cornered race for Governor.
He was a Jackson man and Henry knew it
Though he didn't let James know.

They'd discussed many things when James,
Having been headed off several times,
Finally came straight to the point.
"Wal, Henry, who are you figuring on voting for
In the primary for governor?"

Henry looked off toward the hills.
Then he looked straight at James.
"Wal, I rekon I'll drop my vote fer Aiken—
He's the only one I ain't seen."

Polly Gets No Cracker

Sleighing had held good up to a week before Town Meeting.
Then a warm breeze dropped into the valley
And dissolved the drifts along the roadside
And made large bare spots on the hills.
Jim Vetal viewed the change with some misgivings.
He was drawing four-foot wood for Charlie Bell
And many of the folks in the village were yet to be supplied.
The first day of the thaw Jim had need to snow one piece of road
And he was afraid he'd have to cut down his loads.
The next day he got an early start
Hoping to get a load for Mrs. Miner to the village
Before the warming sun did more damage.
By driving beside the road where he could
He managed to get his good sized load up the hill
Leading into the village.
He stopped at the Miner driveway to look it over.
It was still icy up the silent grade
Almost to the sidewalk which was bare and on either side.
Jim decided if he could get up enough speed he could make it.
While he was getting onto the load and gathering up the reins
Mrs. Miner came out with Loretta, her parrot, in her cage
And hung it on the porch in the sun.
Jim waved his whip at her and then cracked it
As he gave the team the word in a loud voice.
They started up the grade with a mad rush.
It looked as though they'd make it.
But just as the front sled hit the bare spot
Loretta, excited by all the whip cracking and shouting,
Flapping her wings screeched in her highest tone "WHOA."
Mrs. Miner let Jim exercise his profane vocabulary
While he prepared to take off part of his load.
She leaned over the porch rail, her black eyes twinkling.
"Well Jim, that only goes to prove
That it doesn't pay to heed all you hear,
Even if you're just a horse."

Vote Fraud

Henry Bacon had been a Justice in the Borough
For close to thirty years.
He had held various other town offices
And he always took his job seriously.
He was well versed in the law
And he carried out its demands faithfully.
Of course at election time he was always on hand
To count votes as soon as the box was turned.
The voting arrangements were somewhat unusual.
The election was held in the basement of the Town Hall.
Two pieces of scenery were tacked up at an angle along the wall
And the small triangular space thus cut off
Offered some slight privacy for the ballot marker.
Each partition was by a window and the ledge
Offered space for writing.
The ballot box was on an old pulpit
Which had once flourished down at the Corners.
There had been about the usual turnout of voters
And Henry and the other Justices were sitting at the long table
Counting the ballots dumped from the box by the Constable.
Ed Fletcher held a ballot up to get a better light on it.
"By mighty," he said, "somebody musta made a mistake.
Here's a cross top o' the Democrat column."
He passed it around and they all agreed.
After some discussion as to the possibility
That the action was wilful, Henry said to put it aside.
They could get the rest done and then decide what to do.
Pretty soon Henry stopped and looked at a ballot carefully.
He held it out so that all could see.
"I guess that settles it," he said
"Here's another ballot with a cross on the Democrat column."
He looked over his glasses.
"Throw both o' them ballots out.
That son-of-a-gun voted twice."

Threats

Probably Ambrose's "threats"
Started when he was a child.
He was told to do things.
Usually he was also told
What dire thing would befall him
If he failed to obey.

As an older boy—he never really grew up—
He found that threats often served
When he couldn't get his own way
By persuasion or even by rights.

Ambrose and his wife lived on a back road
And thanks to his wife, they were in comfortable circumstances.
They had food enough, a comfortable home,
And there was a little in the savings bank
Which Stella added to, little by little.
Ambrose got more and more to feel
That he wasn't so very important to Stella.
His suggestions were not acted upon as a rule
And he became sullen.
Then one day he made a great discovery.
He had decided not to set up a stove in the parlor.
It wasn't used more than twice all winter
And if the "settin' room wa'n't good enough fer the Minister
He cud stay to hum."
There had been words over the stove question
And Ambrose had announced that he was done.
He strode out across the fields toward the woods.
The group of neighbors had brought him back
After midnight to a trembling and remorseful wife.

Time and again a threat to leave served his purpose.
As it began to fail he hinted at a removal
Which would be final and doubtless bloody.
This had worked several times
When one Spring day, after a period of sullen silence,
He announced to Stella that he was going to the barn
And he added a dark hint as to his purpose.

Two hours later the undertaker drove into the yard.
He spoke in subdued tones as he met Stella at the door.

He put his coat over a chair and started toward the bedroom.
"He ain't in there," Stella said. "He's to the barn."
The undertaker stood with the door half open.
"He went out t' the barn t' hang himself.
That was more'n two hours back.
I reckoned it was time you come."

That was Ambrose's last threat.

Unused Knowledge

When Steve Dill drove up to the hotel
With the two-seated open sleigh he met trains with
He deposited a young man with a small grip.
On the way home from the railroad station
Steve hadn't found out as much as he usually did
About what his passenger's business might be.
"What be you, sellin' suthin', young feller?" he finally asked.
"Trying to," the passenger answered as he started
    toward the hotel.
That afternoon when Steve took the mail into the store
He found the young man talking with two of the setters
Around Brayley's stove, and he joined them.
The young man greeted him as an old acquaintance.
Steve found that farming was under discussion
And he asked the stranger if that was his line.
"Well, in a way, yes it is," the youth said.
Looking him over Steve decided he was a city fellow
Who might be out looking for a farm to buy.
He had to go before he found out what he wanted to know.
In due time the group of setters found out the young man
Was selling a book on scientific farming.
At their suggestion the next morning he hired a cutter
And drove out to see Ellsworth Hines, four miles
    up the mountain.
Ellsworth wasn't much of a farmer
And even if he had been his farm wouldn't have paid.
He was never accused of overexerting himself.
When the young man knocked on the door
Ellsworth was sitting by the kitchen stove reading a paper
While his wife was out hanging up the washing
Which was several days late in getting done.

He welcomed the visitor, made him take his coat off
And listened to his story, interrupting with intelligent questions.
Finally the young man, feeling he was in the right place,
Pulled out his order book and got his pencil ready.
Ellsworth looked up from the book he'd been examining.
"Well now, young man, I know that's an awful good book
And I've enjoyed visitin' with yu, but it wouldn't be
    any use t' me."
The young man looked at Ellsworth in amazement.
"But why not, Mr. Hines? Why wouldn't it?"
Ellsworth dropped his chair onto four legs and stretched.
"Nope," he said. "Ye see I don't farm it half as good
    as I know how
Even as 'tis."

Even Tempered

Some of the older inhabitants
Excused 'Lizy Grayford's temper
On the grounds that she'd lost the man she wanted.
The less charitable ones, mostly those
Who had dealings with 'Lizy,
Accepted this as a reason but not as an excuse.
They agreed with Grandpa Graylord,
The father of the man she did marry.
He often said that a woman like that
Had ought to been most choked to death
When she showed the first symptoms.
"Then," he said "she'd a been dead
Er else it would have scart the cussedness out of her."
He usually added that he'd 'a done some choking
On his son Henry if he'd known he was so dumb
As to have got taken by any such vixen.
The odd thing was she was quite fine looking
And had been something of a belle in her youth.
All of her beaus eventually ran up against her temper
And deserted before it was too late.
It was the temper that seemed to attract Henry.
He liked to handle horses that were too mean for others.
He usually succeeded in taming even the worst of them.
Evidently when he married 'Lizy
He expected to have the same success with her.

As the years went on her temper got worse
And Henry settled down to take his defeat as best he could.
One rainy day in early summer he was sitting in the store
Waiting for 'Lizy to do some trading.
She scolded the storekeeper about his goods
And jumped on him for charging such prices.
She watched the scales when he weighed things
And questioned their accuracy.
Henry picked up her packages and went out with her.
He came back shortly for something she'd found was left out.
He knew the storekeeper was telling the sitters
What he thought of his late customer by their guilty looks.
As he picked up the forgotten package he said:
"Boys, that woman o' mine is the evenest tempered
Of any woman in the valley."
They all looked bewildered and kept silence.
As he got to the door he turned and added:
"Yessir, absolutely even-tempered—
She's mad all the time."

The Professor Takes A Walk

The Professor used to say
That the one thing that made him put up with
Getting older was the fact
That he had grown up to young manhood
During the years when walking was the chief way
People moved from one spot to another;
When pedestrians could journey on the highway
Without danger of sudden death,
Or being made to appear very ungracious,
Or inclined to be a bit crazy
To numerous passing motorists who stopped,
And even backed up several rods to proffer a lift.
To those who had been born too late
To experience the feeling of complete freedom
Travel through the countryside on foot offered,
The Professor delighted in recounting experiences
And even adventures which had befallen him.
Not a few of the encounters which might,
Even to the speed-bred younger generation,
Come under the heading of ADVENTURES

Befell him due to the fact that in those days,
He would remind his young listeners,
There were not numerous signs, as later, along the highways
Announcing TOURISTS ACCOMMODATED,
  or simply GUESTS.
There rest and refreshment might be had
In a great variety of family surroundings.
But invariably where guests were prepared for,
In the good old days of foot use and foot loose,
The spot where one might spend the night
Depended on where that time of day overtook him.
The Professor always held that this very variety
Of types of people and manners of living met with,
Was what added zest to the journey.

This year he'd waited several days for May
To be fairly sure she had moved in to stay.
Pack basket on his back he had been careful
Not to overdo the first few days.
He had stopped to watch a man plowing—
A little late but it was a mountain farm.
There were still a few snow banks by the woods.
He smelled the richness of the new turned earth.
He went on to where the road started down,
And there before him spread the valley.
Nearby the few cleared spots showed brown grass,
But below there were green walled-off meadows,
And along the still full-running brook
He could see here and there shad bush in bloom.
Further down he saw a white house
And he began to think of lodging and a meal.
A boy stood by the barnyard fence
And the Professor, observing a watering trough,
Stopped and asked if he might drink.
The boy smiled and said "Of course."
"Or maybe you'd like a glass of cider."
The Professor met his smile and asked, "Is it good?"
The boy looked up to the mountain. Then he said:
"Guess 'tis. Pa swallowed two tumblers an hour back.
He's back up there now, huntin' a bear
With a buggy whip."

A Midnight Caller

Everything had gone wrong that Friday
And when Ezra Stevens tumbled into bed
He thought he had never been so petered out.
It always happened that way when Bessie, his wife,
Left him to run the farm and do his own housework.
Of course when Bessie had gone she had prepared
Enough of the staples such as bread and a roast of pork
And plenty of doughnuts and cookies
To last, she hoped, until she was back.
The only comforting thought which struggled through
Was that the reason for her going was a grandson.
All the other grandchildren had been girls
And Ezra had longed for a grandson
To carry on the name.
With that thought he blew out the lamp
And tumbled into his bed.
It seemed as though he had just closed his eyes
When he heard a noise and Shep barking.
The noise sounded out toward the highway
Which ran past the house a few rods away.
Ezra turned over and drifted off again.
Then Shep barked furiously and from far off
Ezra heard a pounding noise.
In due time he realized someone was hammering on the door.
He jumped out of bed half awake
He opened the window and looking down
Saw a man on the porch who called to him:
"My car's off the road. Can I get you to haul me out?"
Ezra shouted "I'll be down," and shut the window.
The moon was bright enough so he got into some clothes
And stumbled down the stairs before he lighted a lamp.
He got his lantern and went out to the barn.
Some time later the big Cadillac was in the road.
The man stood there slapping his pockets.
"By George," he said, "I guess I'll have to owe you.
I don't seem to have a cent on me."
Ezra looked at him a minute.
Without a word he hooked onto the car
And pulled it back into the ditch.
Picking up the chain he started toward the house.
"There you are. No need to worry a mite.
You don't owe me a damned cent."

At The Grist Mill

The old stone grist mill
Looked as though it had grown where it stood
A century or so ago between the hill and the river.
Its walls were two feet thick, solid masonry,
And in case of need it might have served
As a fort if such were ever needed
In that peaceful valley.
The water that turned the big wheel
Came from a small pond upstream
Flowing smoothly and quietly, with dignity,
Along its stone walled channel to the power maker.
There it poured in a mad torrent to its task.
There was always the rhythmic swish of the water
As each bucket of the overshot wheel
Emptied its load into the outlet channel below.
This might be drowned out by the rumble
Inside when the mill was busy with its grinding.
Then the miller had to shout to be heard above the roar.
Conversation with his customers generally went on
Outside on the loading platform in summer
And inside the office by the big stove in winter.
Everything was coated with fine white meal dust,
Including Sam Hibbard, the miller.
Several dusty cats were also part of the working force,
But daytimes they usually slept in the office.
They were the night watchmen.
One spring day Sam, the miller,
Saw Frank Monkton in his sagging buckboard
Driving toward the mill.
Frank was generally known as a dead beat.
His name was on the books of every store in town
And the miller had told Joe, his helper, not to trust him.
He stopped at the platform and swung his feet out.
He talked crops and weather and then casually:
"Better drop a hundred o' meal on for me."
He was reaching into his pocket
When Sam dropped the bag on the back of the buckboard.
"That'll be seventy-five cents," Sam said.
"Can you change a twenty?" Frank asked.
His hand was still in his inside pocket.
"Gosh, no," Sam said, taken aback.

His customer withdrew his hand and picked up the reins.
Clucking to the horse he said in parting:
"I was 'fraid y'couldn't,
So I didn't fetch it along."

Mourning Deferred

Of course the conscientious housewives in the neighborhood
Simply couldn't understand Aggie Hood's behavior.
Not that she didn't know how to be a good farm wife.
When she had a mind to she could do as well
As even the most critical could ask.
The thing they could never forgive was her attitude
Toward her husband.
She made life miserable for him at home
And enjoyed criticizing him to any who would listen.
Alfred was not one to take such things sitting down
And the result was a household decidedly divided.
One spring she decided she needed a change, right in sugaring.
So she simply packed her grip and took the stage
To go and visit a sister down in Massachusetts.
She and Alfred had one of their not infrequent "jawings"
But that didn't seem to deter Aggie in the least.
When word came that she was sick
The feelings of sympathy either on the part of the neighbors
Or even of Alfred were entirely lacking.
Both felt that it served her right.
One noon Alfred and the two men helping him in sugaring
Were washing up for dinner when there was a knock at the door.
It was a telegram telling of Aggie's demise.
Alfred read the message slowly, without changing his expression.
He folded it carefully and then stood holding it in his hand.
Then he pulled himself together and said in a
    business-like manner:
"Well, we're jest agoin' t' set down t' dinner."
He stuffed the telegram into his overalls pocket,
And emptied the basin into the sink.
"But," he went on, "when we've et
There'll be the damndest bawlin' around here
Y' ever heered in yer life."

Eliza Catches On

Strangers in the valley often wondered
Why on earth that first generation of Parkinsons
Saw fit to build their house
Away off there miles from anyone,
And at the end of a road which was so steep
As it drew near to the house
That often in winter it had to be abandoned
And a new and longer track made in the snow.
Going back many years it would be found that a road
Used to go a quarter mile back of the house
Following the higher ridge above the valley.
It had long since been abandoned
Leaving only some traces of stone walls to mark it,
With now and then a cellar hole or some apple trees.
Those who made the steep climb to the house
Usually stopped at the top to look back
Where the valley lay, north and south,
Twisting with the river which wandered through it, unhurried,
And felt the exaltation born of high places.
Perhaps that was one reason why Eliza Parkinson
Persisted in living there, the last of her family,
With only the hired man and his wife
And a half century of memories to keep her company.
As she grew older she got more and more dependent
On Doctor Templeton, down in the valley.
After climbing the ascent in all kinds of weather
Only to find nothing really wrong with the old lady,
He finally spoke plainly and told her
She was not to send for him
Unless there was something really wrong—other than loneliness.
It was over a month before the hired man
Appeared one late fall night, with snow in the air,
At the Doctor's door with a message from Eliza.
The man was sure there was something wrong
But he hadn't waited to find out just what.
Reluctantly the Doctor hitched up his horse.

*   *   *   *   *

He could hear her breathing as soon as he opened the door.
She smiled a wan smile when he came into the room.
A week later Eliza was able to sit up in bed.
By then the Doctor knew how she'd fallen into the brook

44

And dislocated her ankle and then managed to crawl
To where she could make the hired man's wife hear.
This morning she said to the Doctor:
"I hope you didn't think I called you this time
For nothing—except loneliness," she added,
Almost in a whisper.
The Doctor swallowed a couple of times and looked away.
Then he said in his usual brusque manner:
"No 'Liza. You caught on all right."
He patted her arm and reached for his case.
"Kinda overdid it, though," he added.

A Dealer In Shorts

Ezra was a man of large frame,
Of medium stature and quite given to hairiness.
His gray hair was getting thin where the part was
But Ezra somehow made what he had go quite a ways.
It was general talk around the village
That Ezra could stretch dollar bills, too.
When it came to stuff he measured or weighed
He usually managed to do some stretching there.
The time his left hand stiffened up
With what at first looked like paralysis
Ned Ketchum asked the doctor if it might not be
"That Ezry's hardened his hand up
Pressin' down on them scales o' hiss'n."
The scales were placed behind all sorts of things
Piled on the front of the counter.
No matter how bright the day
It was always a little shady in Ezra's store.
He always made a good deal of the weighing job
Tipping his head back so he could see
Through the lower part of his glasses.
As he put the weight into the right notch
He'd drop in a few crackers and then take some out,
Or sift a little more sugar in and then scoop some out.
Everybody was sure they were getting short weight
But nobody ever thought of telling Ezra so.
It would have hurt his feelings.
Only one man ever tried to catch Ezra
And that was Old Man Skinner
Who sold cord wood piled so you could throw a cat through it.

Ezra had called his attention to such a pile one winter
And the old man planned on revenge.
He brought his molasses jug in that spring
And followed Ezra into the almost dark back room
Where he kept the cask of molasses
Beside the blue barrel of kerosene.
Ezra drew the molasses into a battered and sticky measure.
When it was within an inch or so of being full
He turned the spigot off, and Old Man Skinner spoke.
"Here, Ezry, yu old skinflint, that ain't full into two inches."
Ezra didn't even look at him as he started pouring it
    into the jug.
"I know that," he said, holding the sticky funnel upright,
"There was an inch er so in th' measure
When I put it under th' spigot."

What Next!

The Howard boy had reported it first
To a skeptical audience sitting on the store steps.
Out of breath and pale through his freckles
He had told them, with no leading up to it,
That Jimmy Hudman had hung himself.
Gradually some of them believed it must be true.
Jimmy had always been taken for granted.
He'd always been a bit queer
But folks remembered his parents
And thought no more about Jimmy.
He'd lived alone in the only roofed part
Of an old house a mile out of the village.
By the time it was certain the news was true
The conscience of the village
Had begun to suffer some pangs.
For the first time most of them realized
What a lonely life Jimmy must have led.
By afternoon the story had spread
And by then there was a general seeking
Of someone to blame for allowing Jimmy to be so neglected.
When Grandma Dickerman, who lived near the top
    of the mountain,
Was told the tragic story
She stopped shelling peas
And shoved her spectacles up on her wrinkled forehead.

"Killed hisself? Jimmy, 'd yu say?"
She cupped her hand behind her ear.
"My lands, you don't say! Killed hisself!
By hangin'? O my goodness gracious, think of that!"
She rocked a minute.
"Well, after all, I can't say I'm much surprised.
You never could tell about Jimmy.
He was all'as up t' somethin'."
She reached for her pan of peas
And shoved her glasses down on her nose.
"Hung hisself," she said as though she was talking to herself.
"Well my goodness gracious,
What will he be up to next?"

Green vs. White

Henry Stoddard lived on the mountain road.
From his back porch he got a view of Vermont mountains
Which he never failed to talk about, given a listening ear.
On one side the Green Mountains flanked the valley.
On the other the marching mountains of the Taconic range
Seemed to be drawing close to the others in the hazy distance.
A single peak far beyond held them apart.
Henry used to sit on the porch after supper
And watch the twilight settle on the waiting valley.
He watched winter storms sweep along the mountain tops
And then drift down to blot out the valley.
Somehow, the sight of those mountains and that reaching valley
Brought peace to Henry's soul.
Or the strength of its storms stirred an answering something
In his blood.
Not that he thought it all out.
He took it into his being as he did breath into his lungs.
One fall, after haying, he went to New Hampshire to visit.
His sister lived where she got a view of the White Mountains.
Henry tried to be complimentary about them but
   he missed something.
One day he came on an artist trying to put on his canvas
Some of the majesty of one of the rugged peaks.
Henry stopped to talk with him.
"I have to soften those mountains a bit,"
The artist said, leaning back to look at his work.
"They're a little harsh, just as they are."

Henry looked at the canvas and then at the mountains.
"Well, you'd better come over into Vermont," he said.
"Save you some trouble—
Th' Almighty softened 'em over there."

The Peg Race

For most of the people on the grandstand
Or crowded as close to the fence as possible
The Peg Race was undiluted fun.
The more trouble the contestants had
In getting their steeds harnessed and away
The better the yelling spectators liked it.
To one of the entrants, however, it was a serious matter.
It was not the few bushels of oats or the horse blanket
Offered as prizes that interested Willie Howe,
What made the event serious for Willie was this:
His horse had once been on the track and had a mark.
He had traded for him over in York state
And had spent most of his summer building him up.
He had also done no little talking to build up his reputation.
There was no question that the beast—Dan J. he called him—
Could step once but now both knees forward were sprung
And his wind was replenished with painful and audible effort.
Willie had always wanted to drive trotting horses.
He had practiced with Dan J. day after day on the track
But during the practice two things now present were missing.
There was no band blasting its loudest
For the very purpose of exciting the horses,
And no crowd trying to make more noise than the band.
These two new conditions were what upset Dan J.'s nerves.
By the time Willie had succeeded in getting him hitched
    to the buggy
All of the other entrants were away and one was half
    around the track.
Willie was not dismayed for it was trotting speed he had to offer.
As the early starters were passing the grandstand on the first lap
Willie was getting the best he could out of Dan J.
On the back stretch a quarter of a mile behind.
As he swept past the yelling crowd alone in his glory
He was still urging his poor steed to show them.
Various methods of increasing his horse's speed

Were offered to the unheeding Willie as he entered the last lap.
He dropped further and further behind.
The others had all passed under the wire
When Willie, still driving as if he were breaking all records,
Came into the home stretch almost forgotten by the crowd.
As he drove under the wire there was a sudden silence
Broken only by the music of the merry-go-round, drifting
    on the wind,
And the far away shouts of the hawkers and showmen.
A penetrating voice from the crowd rang out:
"Never mind, Willie. You've had a nice ride anyhow."

Drawing A Jury

From the time he could manage to skip school
To attend County Court when it met in the Village
Josiah Scroby seemed to enjoy it more than
Any other public doings which demanded no admission fee.
At first probably it was just boyish curiosity.
Even as a grown man he could never have been suspected
Of having a legal mind; in fact his mind was his weak point.
Perhaps it was because of the mystery
Usually connected with matters of a criminal nature.
The mighty dignity of the Judges
And all of the ceremonial doings made some impression,
But probably most of all the heroic deeds of the sheriff
Who moved among criminals without fear;
Who carried on his belt under his coat
A real loaded shooting iron.
When he acquired from a trash heap real law books
He felt he absorbed some of the dignity of the law.

          *   *   *   *   *

The day he was elected a Justice of the Peace
He cleared out the old harness room
And put up a shelf for his unread law books.
A discarded kitchen table became his desk.
His desk chair was a retired rocker, obviously chosen
With an eye on comfort rather than use of the pen.
He'd married two couples when Ambrose Skane,
A town character much addicted to cider,
Was brought before him on a charge of Breach of the Peace.
It was nothing new for Ambrose but this time

He demanded a jury trial and stated he could defend himself.
The office of Judge Scroby was packed that morning.
The proceedings followed no set of rules.
Mighty legal phrases mingled with everyday speech.
Choosing of a jury was difficult since Ambrose, defendant,
As his own attorney, objected as each one was called,
Often on the grounds of prejudice due to acquaintance.
Finally, worn out, Judge Josiah turned to Ambrose.
"Amb—er—Will the defendant look at the jurors, rejected,
And state whether or not he knows more than half of them."
Ambrose looked down at the group, then he said:
"Josi—er—Your Honor, I'd say
That I know more'n th' hull lot put together."

Information Please

When the old Howard Mill,
Which for years had used the power
Of the tumbling brook from West Mountain,
Suddenly grew into a factory controlled by outsiders,
Naturally more and more help was needed.
Gradually, from the old force of twenty or so
It was employing nearly a hundred.
It was no longer a family affair.
Of course members of the Howard family
Saw to it that in the deal they still held
Positions rather than jobs.
The two brothers who had inherited the business
Were competent and young enough
To take over executive positions
And soon were used to private offices.
Eddie, the youngest of the "Boys,"
Ten years younger, was considered lacking
In the usual mannish traits due in part
To being kept from many of the usual occupations
By a mother who delayed too long cutting his curls.
He had a job in the new organization
Which was of minor importance, if any.
He took it seriously and went daily to the mill.
He spent much of his time off pumping new recruits.
Among other feminine traits
Was this streak of personal curiosity

And while the men soon learned to take Eddie
As an amusing bit of underdone male,
And put up with him because of the family connection,
Now and then a man like Daniel Gropper from Vermont,
A recent addition to the force, resented Eddie's prying.
But Eddie persisted to the point that it became a battle.
After futile attempts during the noon hour one day
To find out anything much more than Daniel's name,
Eddie asked him: "What did you do, just before you came
    here to work?"
Daniel, who had usually answered all queries by a grunt,
Or even less, suddenly came to life.
"Et m' breakfast," he snapped.

A Collector

Several teams were standing in front of the church
And others were hitched to the fence.
People were coming out of the open double door
Dressed in their Sunday best.
It was Wednesday, the day of George Stiles funeral.
Most of the people stopped on the church platform
Or gathered in small groups by the steps
Waiting for the procession to come out.
Ed Hargood hurried out and started down the street.
He kept his eyes on the ground
Without as much as a nod to anyone.
Everybody knew he was only there
As a matter of duty as a citizen.
From his usual attitude toward his fellow townsmen
People drew the conclusion that attending their funerals
Would be from a sense of public duty
With no shedding of tears involved.
His collection of grudges was probably the largest in town.
Ike Stockwell overtook Ed part way down the street.
"Thought I wouldn't go to th' buryin' grounds," he said.
"Good place t' invite pneumony," Ed said without looking up.
They walked along in silence.
Then Ike said: "The Reverend spoke very nice of George."
Ed walked on without speaking.
He seemed to be trying to remember something.
Then he gave his left shoulder a twist and said:
"Guess he hadn't never traded cows with 'im."

A Master Carpenter

The sign outside of the house
Was so weather beaten that many of the letters
Had to be guessed at.
It read JAMES OSGOOD, MASTER CARPENTER.
The master carpenter's house was well built
But as a sample of architecture it was a sad medley.
It was on the porch which James had added
That he had let his masterfulness have full play.
It was a nightmare of scrolls, half circles, and gingerbread.
As long as the village residents were his customers
James Osgood was able to use his ideas freely.
When the summer people began to buy up old houses
They found that what they wanted to have done
Had to coincide with James' ideas or it wasn't accomplished.
As he was the only real workman in the village
This often made unpleasant complications.
He was especially averse to keeping the old houses.
His idea was to modernize according to his standards
And it took several trying experiences to make him
    follow instructions.
On small jobs he was able to keep to what he thought right.
When Mrs. Judson left in the fall she told James
To put a railing around her cottage piazza
Since her small boy would be running around the next summer.
When she came back in June the railing was done.
She wasn't satisfied with it
But she didn't dare complain to Mr. James Osgood
When he came over to add a gate across the front steps.
She was quite complimentary under his skillful leadership.
All the morning she kept going out to look at it
Hoping there would be an opening for her critical suggestion.
Finally, as James Osgood was picking up his tools
She asked him if he thought it might be possible
That the upright pieces were just a little too far apart.
"You don't think the baby could crawl out between them
Do you Mr. Osgood? I'm sure he couldn't."
He gave her a look and finished collecting his tools.
As he started off he remarked to the world in general,
"Any young 'un that's spindlin' enough
'T fall through them slats
Ain't wuth raisin'."

An Epidemic

Bare spots were showing
On the south slopes
And water was running
Down the ruts in the road.
Crows were calling from the hills.
There was the feel of Spring in the air.
The stage was moving slowly
Up the hill from the depot to the village.
As the horses splashed through the mud
John was giving the winter's news
To a summer resident
Who had come up early
To see about some changes in his house.
He had learned that their wash lady
Had married again
And that old Andrew Goshen,
Who used to peddle vegetables,
Had passed on.
"Had much of this new disease
They call the Grippe?"
It was the year of the first epidemic.
John turned half around in the driver's seat
"Yes. We had that.
Kep th' doctors hustlin' too,
But that wan't what carried 'em off."
The visitor expressed surprise.
"Nope. We had somethin' worse 'n that.
Four folks died of it that I know of."
"What did they call the disease?"
John clucked to his horses.
Then he said, over his shoulder:
"They called it the Ree-lapse."

A Conduct Censor

Just what started Jimmy Herndon
On his career as village judge
Only a student of his childhood could tell.
He had grown up keeping a good deal to himself
And thereby developing a suspicious attitude.

53

His wife came from over the mountain
And she never made any friends in the new home.
By then Jimmy seemed a middle-aged man.
He had charge of the burying ground
And he did odd jobs around the town.
What he earned together with what he had inherited
Made him comfortably well off for those times.
Jimmy and his wife might have lived very happy lives
But there were too many people doing things
That Jimmy could not approve of.
Not that he ever tried to correct the faults of others;
He simply had little to do with them.
If occasion offered he would express his mind
Especially if something nice had been said about the offenders.
He prided himself on his honesty and frankness.
A favorable opinion of anyone could not be an honest one
So he went on through life critical and unhappy.
Perhaps he had never heard:
"Judge not that ye be not judged."
He was sometimes a little hard of hearing.
When Abel Smithers died Jimmy found only one spot
On the family lot where there was room for a grave.
He hung his coat on the fence and began digging.
He still had two feet or so to go
When he came on a ledge of limestone.
He found the ledge shelved off
So he could dig the head end the proper depth.
He hunted up the selectmen to see what to do with the ledge.
They decided it couldn't be blasted nor could it be broken out.
So it was left with one end two feet lower than the other.
After the service, as Jimmy was about to begin his work
The minister looked down at the slanting coffin.
"It seems too bad to leave things like that," he said.
Jimmy who had long had his opinion of the deceased
Leaned on his spade and gave final judgment.
"He wa'n't never on the level.
He certainly wa'n't what you'd call an upright man.
It seems t' me he sets jest as he's suited to."

A Faith Cure

George Huggins' mother had been bed-ridden for twelve years.
She liked to go over her symptoms the time she was "taken,"
All the details leading up to her feeling queer
With the pains in her head and the numb feeling in her limbs.
She had tried all three of the town's doctors,
Taking the medicine of one for a while and then switching.
The fact that her son never paid any of them
Except with a little farm produce, when they became insistent,
Didn't in the least interfere with her demands on them.
When the new doctor came to take Dr. Evans' place—
Dr. Evans had moved to a larger town—
She sent for him at once.
She had a glorious half hour telling him all her symptoms.
He called regularly for some weeks
And then she suddenly dismissed him.
She had read of a mail order cure
Meant for cases just like hers.
Thousands had been made well by this wonderful discovery.
The new doctor sent his bill to George.
He was more businesslike than the older practitioners
And he sent in his bill again and again.
Finally he threatened to sue.
It was then that George transferred his property to his wife.
That fall the case came into court.
The Judge decided that the transfer of property,
Evidently made to avoid attachment, would not hold.
The old lady, lying in her bedroom off the kitchen
Heard her son come in and announce to his wife
That "that crook of a Judge" had declared against him.
She called from her bed:
"Fetch me m' clothes."
Before they could stop her she was up.
Shaking with rage she somehow got into her dress.
Her unused legs would hardly support her
But she managed to hobble out into the kitchen.
"I'll show them doctors they can't bamboozle me,"
She screamed in a high piping voice.
And she lived to be past ninety
And sewed carpet rags
Two days before she died.

Winter In The Valley

The white blanket which covered the valley
Showed the wrinkles of a restless night.
Wherever there was anything to stop the wind-driven snow
Drifts had piled up sometimes ten feet deep.
Though the sun was out frequent gusts
Filled the air with blinding clouds.
Two men with plows fastened to the runners of a bob sled
Were struggling toward the village trying to open the road.
Jim Shepard was making his way from his farm above the valley.
He had a tippet tied around his head over his cap.
When a gust came along he turned his back to it
Leaning against it as though it was something solid.
When it let up he found himself off balance.
He finally got to the store.
He stopped outside to brush the snow from his moccasins.
As soon as he got inside he unwound the tippet
And got his ears out from under his cap so he could hear.
"Tough day," he said to the storekeeper as he cut off a chew.
The storekeeper, glad of some company, drew his chair up.
"Yes 'tiz. How's th' goin'? D'je drive in?"
"Take a horse out a day like this?" Jim said.
"Well I guess not s'long as I can shake a leg."
The storekeeper said he was more considerate
Of his animals than he'd be.
Jim got the range of the box of sawdust.
"You're jest like my woman," he said.
"She was complainin' th' other day 'cause I wouldn't hitch up
And take her to some female doins to th' Center.
She sez to me 'You think more o' that mare
Than yu do o' me,' she sez."
Jim chewed a minute.
"I sez t' her, I sez, 'Look here old lady
If you'd crinkle up your nose and whinner,
Ev'ry time I come 'round th' way th' old mare does,
Mebbe I'd think more o' you, by gosh,' I sez."

Jed Gets In His Wood

Jed had lived his fifty-odd years in the village.
From the time he was a small boy he stole.
Of course as a boy he was now and then caught red-handed.
By the time he was in his twenties
He was more particular about what he stole and when.
He confined his efforts to filching things from gardens
Or now and then grabbing a fowl about right for the pot.
Any time anything was missing, Jed was suspected.
Nobody ever took the pains to track him down.
The fact of the matter was nobody wanted to come out
And have a trial and Jed sent to jail
Over a matter of a few vegetables or a chicken.
Besides with Jed out of the way who'd there be
To blame when something turned up missing.

Last winter Ed Williams heard somebody was cutting wood
On his prize woodlot on the mountain.
Of course Ed thought of Jed right off
But it looked like too much of a job for Jed.
One day he went up to the lot to find out for sure.
He ran right onto Jed loading pole wood.
He'd borrowed the dray and team from a neighbor.
The righteous indignation which had been accumulating
All through the years in Ed's mind
Suddenly had a legitimate outlet.
He tried to speak naturally but his voice sounded queer.
"What the idear, you cuttin' and haulin' off my wood?"
Jed looked more pained than surprised.
He gazed at Ed and chewed slowly.
Then he seemed to get the idea.
He turned to spit.
"I guess you're right Ed. I hadn't orter done it."
He gained confidence as he went on.
"It's your wood and I ain't no business with it.
I'd orter let it alone."
He looked down and poked a chip with his foot.
Ed was figuring how much Jed had taken
And how he could get anything out of him for it.
Jed looked up and spoke with decision:
"I'll tell you Ed, you jest help me pile on these few sticks
And we'll call that th' end of it."

Dazed at the sudden reversal of affairs
Ed took hold mechanically and before he realized it
Jed and the wood were disappearing down the snowy track.

Work Units

Sirenus would never have hired Joe
If haying hadn't come on with such a rush.
The spring had been rainy and backward
But the grass had a good start.
By early July when the weather turned hot
It was ready for cutting all at once.
Joe had showed up one evening
When Sirenus had a lot of hay down
And everybody was worn out with the heat.
He took Joe on even though he showed signs
Of having been on a good long spree.
Sirenus' wife knew she could smell "spirits" on him
But she was willing to put up with even that.
Joe's lack of interest in his job
And his frequent stops to drink from the water jug,
Usually accompanied by a spell of resting on his scythe,
Was excused on the grounds that he wasn't quite sobered up.
When he found more and more chances to loaf
As the week went on Sirenus' temper began to stir.
He gave him several warnings but Joe paid no attention.
By Friday Sirenus had stood as much as he could.
He paid Joe off and advised him to move rapidly.
Along toward the end of the next week
Sirenus was cutting the meadow next to Rob Howe's.
Rob happened to be working on his field the same day
And they stopped by the stone wall to visit a minute.
To Sirenus' surprise he saw his late hired man
Driving the horse rake in his neighbor's meadow.
He was about to get back to his mowing
When Rob nodded in the direction of Joe
Who had stopped the horse under the shade of a tree.
"D'ju git any work out o' that feller?"
Sirenus appeared to notice Joe for the first time.
"Yes, some," he said, looking at Joe.
Rob gathered up his reins.
"Y' got all they was," he said, as the team started.

Political Science

When Libby Hatch went to work
In Mis' Tromley's COMEETA LUNCH
Some of the village folks thought she wouldn't do.
They didn't have anything against Libby
But they didn't think she had the gray matter
To remember orders and to make change.
At first she did try Mis' Tromley's patience
By getting generally mixed up.
But after a few weeks she was doing very well
And the customers put up with her failings.
There were three kitchen tables covered with oilcloth
In a row against the south wall,
Four good hard kitchen chairs to each.
The usual sugar bowl, salt and peppers, vinegar cruet
    and glass for toothpicks
Libby kept full and the oilcloth she kept clean.
There was usually one dinner menu each day
And regulars knew just what to expect
On any particular day of the week.
In the partition at the back there was a window
Through which Mis' Tromley passed the food.
It was always piping hot and well seasoned
And there was always a good sized helping.
Libby liked to call the order through the window
And since Mis' Tromley wasn't seen
Libby got to feel she was running the place now and then.
When the proprietor did come out
It would be when business was confined to one or two parties,
Generally people she knew, and she'd draw up a chair
And likely sip a bit of tea.
Meanwhile town gossip was hashed over.
One day Kingdom Read stopped in as was his habit.
He lived up the valley and sold feed and grain.
Shortly he told Libby he was in the Legislature.
"Well my goodness! You'd ought t' make a good one," she said.
"Wouldn't never get elected here though."
Kingdom pushed his chair back and reached for a toothpick.
"Why not?" he asked.
"No," she said starting to gather up the dishes.
"Here they don't send them as has the most brains—
They just send the man that gits th' most votes."

Confession

Jonas was an easy confessor.
Each year when the revival meetings
Gave folks something to talk about,
Jonas confessed to many sins.
He wasn't a bad man really,
But he seemed to feel
That he needed something
To give him position in the community.
So each year he told how mean he had been;
How he had cheated in business;
How he had lied and deceived.
He made himself out to be
Quite an interesting old sinner.
He was really too timid
To wander far from the straight path.
If anyone had accused him to his face
Of the sins he publicly confessed
He would have been hurt and angry.
One night he had been going over his list
In the last meeting of the fall revival.
He had been cheered on
By frequent amens and hallelujahs,
So that he had painted a blacker portrait
Of himself than he usually did.
Ed Simpson had stopped in
Hoping for a chance to see Ella Lampson home—
She played the melodian.
He was never serious for long
And Jonas' confession was too much of a temptation.
He slowly arose. He was greeted by the exhorter
As a welcome recruit
And urged to give his testimony.
"All I www wants tto say,"
He stammered under excitement,
"Is ttthat II've lived nnnext t' Jonas
Nigh onto forty year
And every wwword he sssays 'bout himself
Is tttrue. Tttthat's mmmy testimony."

A Tailboard Outlook

If it hadn't been for Ezra Tute's woodlot
Probably his farm would have been handed over
  to the mortgagee
Or else sold for taxes.
There wasn't an acre free from outcropping ledges
And his cows wore themselves out hunting for feed
In what passed for pasture land.
He managed to get enough food for himself and his family
But cash crops were something he knew nothing about.
Every winter he sold wood down in the village.
He had a team of uncertain age
Which in winter looked a lot worse than it was.
He never spent much time on its personal appearance
But he never neglected to feed plenty of hay
And as much grain as he could manage to get.
He had a wagon box which he put on a pair of traverses
Made with fairly high sides for wood drawing.
One day he had delivered a load of wood in the village
And he stopped in at the Tavern to refresh himself.
From there he went to the grist mill.
The warmth of the big stove in the mill office
Shortly disclosed that Ezra had stayed too long at theTavern.
The miller put on his two bags of meal for him
And then let him doze by the fire.
Finally he roused Ezra and advised him to get started
If he wanted to get home before dark.
Ezra came to life slowly.
He finally got to his feet and pulled his cap over one ear.
Seeing he could navigate fairly well
The miller went on with his business.
Coming back a little later into the office
The miller heard someone shouting outside.
He went out and there he found Ezra.
He was standing in the rear of the sled box
With his back to the team,
Looking with uncertain gaze on the ground
  beyond the tailboard.
"Shay," he said when he finally located the miller,
"What m' goin' t' do?
Shomebody's stole m' team."

An Early Match

Miss Allenby, who inherited her father's farm,
Came down into the village every Saturday.
She always drove the white horse and rode in the buckboard.
The harness was shabby and one blinder hung out
Like a swinging shutter on a house.
The buckboard sagged with the memory
Of her father's ponderous frame.
As the old white horse jogged along the dusty road
The buckboard wheels rattled on every stone.
Miss Allenby sat on the seat erect and looking straight ahead.
She wore her black dress and the bonnet with jet on it
And she wore black cotton gloves on her gnarled hands.
The general dilapidation of her conveyance
Detracted not one whit from her dignity.
From the way people spoke to her it was evident
That she was received at her own estimation.
Brayley, the storekeeper was never awed by her.
He always accepted her cool aloofness with a twinkle.
One day, after Miss Allenby had done her trading
And was putting her father's long wallet
Back within the secret recesses of her petticoat,
Brayley pulled something out from under the counter.
It was a strip of the new sulphur matches.
Brayley broke one off and scratched it on the seat of his pants.
He held it up as it simmered and sent off sulphur fumes.
Then the wood caught and there was a clear yellow flame.
He gave a sales talk to Miss Allenby telling how simple it was.
She could let the fire go out now if she wanted to
Then simply break off a match, swish, and there was fire.
Miss Allenby bought a half dozen and started home.
The next Saturday she was again in Brayley's store.
She fished out the matches, each one separated from the bunch.
"You can take those useless things back," she said,
"Not a spark could I get out of one of 'em."
Brayley took one, looked at it, and then, swoosh!
He scratched it on the now lined spot in his baggy pants.
A small yellow flame burst into being.
He tried another, holding it out so it would shine clearly.
Miss Allenby looked at it for a minute. Then she said:
"You can keep the pesky, new-fangled, useless things.
If you think I'm coming clear down here to use your trousers

Every time I want a light you're very much
    mistaken, Mr. Brayley.
I shall stick to the good old reliable flint."

The Meat Man

George Ebbets drove the meat cart
For Henry Squires.
The cart was covered with canvas
Which was white once.
It was a sort of prairie schooner
On a small scale.
Henry was so tall he used to have trouble
In tucking his head inside the top.
His feet always hung out
On one side of the thills.
One spring day
He was passing the corner by the store
When one wheel sank deep into the mud.
The horse stopped:
Then he gave a yank.
It was too much for the old harness
And a tug broke.
George was standing beside the horse
Looking at the wrecked tug
And scratching his curly head.
Harley Jameson was loafing in the store
And he happened to look out just then.
He took in the situation at once.
Going to the door
He opened it just a crack.
Then he yelled to Henry:
"Nevah mind Hen.
Jest reach into your caht there
And hitch on one o' your best steaks.
They're tough enough t' pull any load."

Jenny's Town Office

Jenny Colton didn't carry out the usual idea
That laughter is the expression of pleasure.
At least Jenny seemed to get joy out of tears.
When you stopped to think of it
You realized that you'd never heard Jenny laugh.
She did have a smile and it was a rather nice smile
But it most often was the prelude for tears.
Maybe the muscular efforts which change the face into a smile
Pressed on the tear ducts in Jenny's eyes.
The general impression, however, was not that.
It was accepted by the village as a mark of past sorrow.
She gave the impression that this was a vale of tears
And that she had in times past explored its dark depths
So that the memories could never be kept back.
You and all the rest might find cause for joy and laughter.
She would be the last one to gainsay your right to it.
But just the sight of your enjoyment caused a silent seepage
From the full wells of Jenny's ever-ready eyes.
When she grasped the hand of the bride and wished her joy
Her other hand was moving toward her eyes
Already starting to overflow.
Of course she attended every funeral in the village
Equipped with a supply of white handkerchiefs.
No matter who had died the last rites were always accompanied
By a gentle flow from Jenny's generous eyes.
It was after one of these occasions that a few of the bearers
Were gathered about the stove in Braylcy's store.
They were somewhat ill at ease in their best clothes.
One of them was in the act of unbuttoning his stiff collar
Having already put his ready-made tie into his pocket.
"Well," he said as he stretched his cramped neck,
"I hope Jenny Colton's still able t' go t' funerals
When my time comes."
He got further relief by unbuttoning the collar band of
    his stiff shirt.
"If it should happen in a dry time
I'd be sure o' bein' able t' float 'cross th' river."
Brayley leaned over to open the front draft.
"O well," he said, "Jenny's all right,
She's our Town Crier."

All In The Family

Will Patcher was going fishing.
The willows and dogwood were so thick
Along the banks of the Battenkill
That he decided to get George Stone
To take him down in a boat.
It was a cloudy June day
With mist hanging on the mountains
And a warm south wind blowing—
Just enough to make small ripples
On the deep pools.
George Stone was waiting at the river
With an old flat bottom boat.
He had brought a boy along
To help with the oars
So that he could do some fishing himself.
Will Patcher, who was from the city,
Loaded in the rods and a generous lunch,
For they planned to make a day of it.
Slowly they drifted down stream
The boy keeping the boat midstream
Allowing them to cast on either side.
Late that afternoon they landed
Below the Sunderland bridge
With their baskets well filled.
Patcher had a team waiting
And they drove up the valley
To the village just at dusk.
Getting out at the hotel
Patcher gave George a five dollar bill
For his day's work.
George began to fumble in his pockets.
"Guess we bedder gibe the boy subthin', Will."
"Of course, of course."
And Will handed him a dollar.
It wasn't until some days later
That Patcher found out
The boy was George's own son.

Hedridity

All of Josiah Williams' children—
There were eight of them—
Had settled down to honest toil
Except Alfred.
He was now past twenty-five
Yet he showed no signs
Of sticking to any job.
He might work well for several months
And then he would suddenly leave.
He had travelled South and West
Sometimes staying away a year.
He always earned good pay
Wherever he was being handy at anything.
He wasn't wild and he wasn't lazy.
He just had to move every so often.

He had suddenly appeared in town
After a winter in Florida
And his wandering ways were under discussion
One rainy day, at the blacksmith shop.
"Funny," George Speed was talking.
"His folks ain't that way.
There ain't a steadier, harder workin' farmer
Than Josiah. He stuck right here
And carried on that farm
His father left him."
George filled his corn cob.
"Funny 'bout Alfred," he continued.
"Aint nothin' bad 'bout him
But he won't stick to nothin'.
He's jest like a gypsy."
Old man Henderson leaned forward.
"Never knew his Grandpa did ye?
Used t' be a sailor.
He married Ella Summers and settled down.
Well sir, after their two young 'uns come,
Didn't the sea git to callin' him
And off he went. Gone six months er more.
Then he come back and stayed till he died."
He picked up his cane and got onto his feet.
"Alfred's jest like Grandpa Williams.
I tell ye, ye can't go back on this hedridity."

Summer Boarders

Mrs. Higgleby had "taken" a few people
Who wanted to spend a summer on a farm.
After her husband died she decided to expand.
She had a sign painted with HILLTOP on it.
Each season the same families came back
And added people they recommended.
Then late one summer Mrs. Priestly Sniffer arrived.
Ed Bowker the man who drove the bus to the station
Found her on the platform after the Flyer left.
She asked about places to stay for a week.
Ed looked her over and decided the Central House
Would not be up to her style.
Then he thought of Mrs. Higgleby's, and took a chance.
Mrs. Higgleby would ordinarily have refused point blank
As soon as she saw her long painted nails.
One of her regulars had gone unexpectedly, however,
And her interest in the income overcame her prejudice.
She knew she'd made a mistake
As soon as the newcomer came down to supper.
She complained about the lack of bathing facilities.
Mrs. Higgleby was angry at once.
The putting in of the one bathroom, she felt,
Had given her establishment an especial standing.
As if that wasn't enough to bear,
Etta, the girl who did the passing in the dining room
Reported after supper that this woman
Had asked her to bring her breakfast up at eight-thirty.
Then Mrs. Higgleby, hot and flushed from standing
    over the stove,
Decided that she would settle matters.
She marched out onto the porch where the offender
Was sitting aloof from the rest of the boarders.
She stood in front of her and squared off.
She told her what she thought of her desire for a private bath.
She let her know she noted she hadn't relished her supper.
She'd even sent out for bread instead of the hot johnnycake.
"And now my girl says somethin' about fetchin' your breakfast."
Mrs. Higgleby was reaching the climax of her declaration.
"I want t' tell you our folks eat breakfast in th' dinin' room.
We ain't never and we don't callate t' serve no bed eaters,
Not as long as I'm a-runnin' this house."

When Henry Was Laid Away

Probably Henry's place had not seen such a gathering
In all of the seventy-some years it had been Henry's home.
Of course when his father was buried
There was a big turn out
But he had been buried from the church.
Henry hadn't been connected with the church
Or with any other public thing in the valley.
The people climbing the hill by team and on foot
Were many of them going there for the first time.
They were curious about the place
That had always had the air of not being lived in.
Then too it was a pleasant, warm Sunday afternoon
And Henry's funeral offered something to go to.
At the door many of the men stopped
Allowing the womenfolk to go into the darkened parlor
Or sit in the sitting-room.
Some of the men gathered in the kitchen
Where Henry's overalls and jumpers still hung
From the row of hooks back of the stove.
The kitchen fire was almost out but the tea kettle
Was still sending out a thin stream of steam—
A last sign of the life that had gone on
For well toward a century in that cooking-soaked room.
Several of the men gladly realizing that the house was full
Settled down under a tree near the parlor window.
They got interested in talking about their cattle
And their voices rose from subdued funereal to natural pitch.
Suddenly Harvey Tyler, a relative of Henry's,
Stuck his head out of the open window.
In a voice that carried he said:
"Say, if you damned hoss traders
'Ll shut yer cussed mouths fer a few minutes
We'll try t' git a little religion
A-goin' in here."

Aunt Annie

Seymour Stillson was the undertaker.
He was always properly solemn
On occasions demanding his services.
At all other times
There was nothing he loved more
Than getting a joke on someone.
However, he seemed to enjoy it
Even when the laugh was on him.
And he'd hustle down to Graves' store
To tell all about it.
Aunt Annie Bowen
Lived on the same street.
She was small and bent with age,
But her eyes were bright.
She was hurrying home
Using her umbrella for a cane.
It had looked like rain all day
And now the robins were calling
And the wind was damp.
She met Seymour starting down street.
"Better go git your umbrell', Seymour,
It's goin' to rain sure as preachin'."
Seymour looked at the threatening sky.
"Well Auntie, I'm neither sugar nor salt.
Water won't hurt me."
Aunt Annie turned.
She put her bent finger on Seymour's head.
"Seymour, too much water
Don't do dough no good."
Then she chuckled and hurried on.

Cal Has To Slow Up

Cal Lovell lived down by the river.
Because he knew every twist and turn
And all of the best fishing holes
He made a little each summer acting as fishing guide.
As people began to buy summer places in the village
Cal got jobs making garden or mowing lawns,
Though he felt lawn mowing was beneath his dignity.

It was not a skilled occupation
Like gardening or fishing.
Now and then he would do a little job of mason work
Or some carpentering but usually such work
Required too steady application.
He would rarely let on that he knew anything
 about such things.
He would sometimes deliver the washings his wife took in
But he always tried to make it appear
That doing such work was simply one of her hobbies.
That it had any place in the family economy
He would never allow to be suggested.
One summer he had been out of kilter.
He'd had a grippy cold in the winter
And it had hung on with a cough
Which Cal found it worth while to make the most of.
It aroused the sympathy of his summer employers
So that he was able to get considerable resting done
While he was drawing pay as a gardener.
One of the women who employed him was always sympathetic.
Cal had frequently been moved to tears in telling her
Of some of the family troubles during the winter.
When he had demonstrated his cough to her,
The first time he went to her place to work in the spring,
She was full of solicitude over his welfare.
"You just take it easy, Mr. Lovell," she told him.
"Be very careful about getting over-heated
And then sitting where there is a draft."
Cal rested on his hoe and shoved his hat back.
"No need 't worry, Miss.
I ain't callatin' t' work hard enough t' sweat none,
Not in my condition."

A Predicament

The road wound down the mountain
Following the rocky brook.
Near the foot of the last grade
There was a sharp turn
Just after the last bridge was crossed.
Alfred Stevenson had driven that road
A good many times each year
And he knew each twist and turn.

He used to boast about the loads
Of logs he drew off that mountain.
He was inclined to boast about everything
He ever did or had.
His team was always the best in the village
And he intimated that he alone
Could handle such a team.
He made the turn near the foot of the mountain
A little too fast one day,
And the load turned over.
There lay the horses
Flat on their backs,
Their legs waving in the air.
Alfred had jumped off
And stood above the team.
Then he addressed the horses
In his usual ponderous fashion.
"Well now look where you be,
You're in a d—d nice predicament
Fer drawin' a load,
Ain't ye now?"

George Stone, Cobbler

At one time George Stone
Ran a cobbler's shop.
He used to sit on his low bench,
With the round leather seat,
And the last between his knees,
Repairing leather boots.
On the wall hung wooden lasts
Making a catalog of the feet
Of those who patronized George.
A man would have two pairs of boots,
One for wear on special occasions
The other pair for ordinary wear.
When these everyday ones got past repair
The Sunday ones would become everyday ones
And George would have a job
Making a new pair of boots for "best."
One day William Ludlum came in
With a pair of boots for repair.
They certainly needed it

But William never spent a cent
Until he had to, even to save two cents.
He handed the boots over to George,
Who looked them over from heel to toe.
He shook his head.
"Bad shabe, William."
After some talk
William said to George:
"Well, fix 'em up somehow.
Do with 'em jest ez though they was yourn."
George went over them again.
Then he walked slowly to the stove
And, opening the door,
Thrust them into the hot flames.
"Thad's just whad Id'a done
If they was mine, William."

A Dry

Joel Bassett was a temperance crank.
He never drank anything stronger
Than the water from his well
And he used every chance he had
To quote the Scripture
As the final warning
To those who looked on the wine
When it was red.
Early one evening Joel was driving
Along the river road.
Lance Howard was some distance ahead
In such a state of intoxication
That he had to rest against the fence
At frequent intervals.
Joel came around a bend in the road
Just as Lance leaned against a fence
Which wasn't there.
Wholly unsuspecting as to the cause
Of Lance's downfall,
Joel urged his horse ahead
And climbed out of his buggy
To give assistance.
He tried to rouse Lance

Who only muttered.
Then he decided to put him
In his buggy and take him to the doctor's.
As he put his arms under Lance's shoulders
His temperate nostrils were suddenly assailed
By the fumes of alcohol.
With a grunt of disgust
He dropped him.
As he turned to his buggy
He growled at the prostrate form:
"You kin stay there.
You'll keep."

Going To War

John Jadwin wasn't really bad,
He just had something inside
Which demanded expression.
He was generally considered
A plain nuisance—
He was awkward in the way he expressed himself.
At school he had made some progress
Having learned to read and write
Between punishments.
The strange thing about him was
That he never seemed to get any fun
Out of his deviltry.
He naturally took to drink
And hard cider was easy to get.
He had been a problem to the village
For some years
When the call came from Washington
For volunteers.
A group of men too old to go
Was standing on the porch of the post office
Discussing the battle news.
Just then the postmaster came out
With a mail sack for the stage.
"Wal, I hear young Jadwin's enlisted."
Having given his news
He hooked his hands into his galluses
And waited for the comments.

Old Uncle Ezra was leaning against a post
And gazed at the far mountains.
Then he said very quietly:
"I can't think of anybody
We kin get along without any better."

Village Improvement

Jehial Raymond was a land owner.
His great passion in life
Was to own land—
More land.
If he sold an acre—
He always got a good price.
He'd buy several acres
Where land was cheaper.
It wasn't many years
Before the town found
That he owned most of the best land
On all sides of the village,
And considerable on the main street.
When people wanted to buy
They had to pay his price.
Of course he wasn't popular.
He often talked of helping the town
By leaving something handsome
When he died.
He never did much
To keep the town from dying
Before he did.
One morning he met Jim Sykes
Limping along on his two canes.
"Jim, I've been wondering.
I expect t' do suthin' handsome
Fer this old town in m' will,
But I been wonderin' what I cud do
T' kinder improve it now."
Jim looked at him
From beneath his bushy eyebrows.
He leaned on his canes and started off.
"Die, gol darn ye, die,"
He snapped.

Fishing Through The Ice

For several days some of the "boys"
Had been up the valley fishing in Putnam's Pond.
The ice had just got thick enough to hold
And some fairly good catches had been reported.
Saturday it was too cold for fishing and some of the fishermen
Were going over their experiences real and
    imaginary at Brayley's.
Bill Wiggins came in and leaned over the stove
To thaw the icicles from his whiskers.
When the fish stories seemed to have run out
Bill was thoroughly thawed out and he offered his.
"'Bout ten er mebbe fifteen year ago come Feb'rary,
I went fishin' down to the river in what we called the
    'Swimmin' Hole.'
It ain't there now, filled up by freshets I guess,
But it used t' be a tarnation deep hole.
That day 'twas some b'low zero when I set out.
Ice was 'round fifteen inches thick as I recall er mebbe twenty.
I chopped me a hole 'bout a foot er so acrost.
I baited up m' hook with a chunk o' salt pork and
    dropped her in."
Bill paused to squeeze the remaining ice water from his whiskers.
"It went down around ten foot er mebbe ten and a half.
I got a bite and pulled th' critter in.
Baited up again and this time it hadn't gone down
    more'n four foot
When I gut me another bite and I pulled him in.
Wal, sir, next time I just got m' hook baited
And a tarnation good one jumped right out th' hole fer it."
Bill let that sink in while he leaned back in his chair.
"I kicked that 'un off onto th' ice and from then on
I jest held that bait up over th' hole.
Them fish kep' ajumpin' and I kep' akickin' 'em t' one side.
By gosh inside half er mebbe three-quarters of an hour
I musta had near two cartloads laying there on th' ice."
Bill arose and picked up his mittens.
"'Twa'n't what you'd call a good day fer fish neither,"
He said as he started for the door.

A Heavyweight

Hiram was a small man.
Perhaps if he had married
Someone else he might not have seemed so.
But Ella Judson would dwarf any man.
She just made Hiram seem
To shrink and shrink as he grew older.
Perhaps his meekness
Made him seem small, too.
His manner was always apologetic,
Especially when Ella was with him—
And she rarely let him off the farm alone.
Their daughter naturally "favored her Ma."
She was always fat
And at seventeen she weighed three hundred.
Poor Hiram, with these two women,
Looked like the exclamation point
Which their presence always seemed to demand.
Finally the daughter
Got a position in a side show.
Her mother told the news
With true maternal pride.
It was apparent that she
Had not inherited her "talent" from Hiram.
Hiram had taken the daughter to the train
And was standing by the buggy
Watching the last car disappear
Around the curve toward the big world.
He was surprised to feel a queer lump
In his throat.
"Well Hi'm, yer girl ough t' succeed."
Hiram put his blue bandana back in his pocket.
"Yes, yes, I wrote the feller
That runs the side show,
That I'd fetch her to the train."
He grinned and looked around.
"I told him I'd hev t' make two trips."

Good Investment

There had been considerable excitement in the village
When Zenos Hull bought the old Hunt place.
It had been empty so long—
Captain Hunt had died ten years before—
That people couldn't get used to seeing lights there.
Having the bush-covered fence cleared away
And the yard cleaned up gave the street a changed appearance.
Then having Zenos, who had lived all his life on a farm,
Changing all his ways of life at his age, seemed strange.
Mis' Howell who lived across the road
Wondered how it seemed to Zenos to have people walking past
And to be able to walk to the store and post office.
She spent quite a bit of her time,
The first few weeks after the arrival of her new neighbor,
Sitting in her lampless parlor watching the newly lighted house.
Zenos had always lived so far back from a road
That he never thought of pulling the shades down in
   his sitting room.
She found he liked to sit by the stove and rock.
At first he seemed restless.
He'd get up and go out into the kitchen frequently,
Carrying the lamp in his hand.
Then he'd come to the front door and look out.
There was always a column of smoke coming from his chimney
When Mis' Howell, in the morning, her hair in curl papers,
Pulled up her shades on her way to start her kitchen fire.
She was anxious to see how Zenos had fixed things inside
But when she took some hot biscuits to the door,
One of the first nights after he'd moved in,
He never suggested that she come any further.
Of course it wouldn't have seemed right for her,
   an unmarried woman,
To call on him, a widower, even if he was over seventy.
She was telling one of her relatives about Zenos.
He was a cousin by marriage and came from over the mountain.
He'd noticed the change in the Hunt place
And asked her who was living there.
"What's he do?" he asked.
Mis' Howell looked toward his house.
"He don't do anything," she said. "He's retired."
"How'd he ever git enough t' retire on from farmin'?"

The cousin was a farmer himself.
Mis' Howell stopped rocking.
"He didn't. He's buried two wives."
She started rocking again and added: "Made money on
both of 'em."

The Marshall

Sidney had not gone to the war—
Just why, people had forgotten—
Yet each Memorial Day he wore an army hat
And a blue suit
And somehow managed to get in the procession
Which marched to the old grave yard
On the hill outside the town.
He loved the habiliments of war
Though he never showed any signs of being a fighter.
Each year the town had a country fair
On the grounds by the creek.
There were small exhibits of cattle,
Pulling contests of oxen
And chiefly an all day dance.
On a raised platform with flags in each corner
All day the fiddler sawed away
While the dancers "balanced corners"
And "swung their partners."
This year Sid appointed himself Marshall
And in a faded Prince Albert and the army hat
With a sash of red calico around his waist
Astride a white farm horse
He led the band onto the grounds
With all the dignity of a general.
Late in the afternoon, excited with too much orchard tea
He danced wildly while his steed wandered about
Cropping the grass.
Just as the sun was going down below the mountain
Ellie, his spouse, captured him.
And dragging the white steed behind
Led him meekly up the hill,
His brave red sash tucked under his arm.
"Ellie, my dear," he said half crying
"Every dog's got t' have his day."
"Hump, Sid Collins. Soon ez we git home
You'll git yer bone."

Poor Corn Weather

Jared's luck had never been very good.
That fact combined with an uncanny ability
To plant heavily of any crop on the particular year
When prices for it were far below the cost of raising,
Made his failure as a farmer pretty certain.
Much of Jared's planning was done
By using hindsight instead of foresight.
One year the season had been unusually late
And the place he planned to put his corn
Was under water when it should have been planted.
He had managed finally to get the seed in
But then the weather turned cold so it didn't sprout.
At last some sickly yellow leaves poked through.
This time Jared's bad luck
Was not as noticeable as usual
Because nobody in the valley had any better success.
Jared seemed to be a little disappointed.
He had lost some of his distinction.

Finally nature relented somewhat
And the sun shone long enough to give the corn a start.
It was backward but it showed signs of life.
But Jared's land was naturally wet
And every few days there was a downpour.
His corn land never got a chance to dry out.
One Sunday Brayley drove along by Jared's place.
He saw Jared leaning on the fence and stopped.
The unusual weather came in for comment
And that naturally led Jared around to crops.
Brayley spoke optimistically.
This aroused Jared's ire.
"Well, mebbe there's some that natur' smiles on.
They usually is, but I ain't one of 'em."
He waved his hand in the direction of his pallid corn.
"Look at that corn.
Look at it!
By judast priest, when it's ready fer harvestin'
A toad'll be able t' set and eat th' tossels
Without unspringin' his legs."

Scenery

From the climbing road
Green fields swept down
To the river which slowly twisted
Through the narrow valley.
In the distance the mountains
Drew together
In the haze of a warm May day.
Above, the road wound,
Slowly climbing to the summit
Where a church spire
Stood out against the sky.
An old Ford "Coop"
Came around the bend
Where the distant mountains showed.
It wavered uncertainly
And then ran off the road.
It leaned against the bank
With hardly a jolt.
The old people were not hurt,
But they were pale
And the man's voice shook.
"Nope," he quavered
"Nothin' broke. Wan't no fault
With th' machine."
He wiped his brow with a blue handkerchief.
He made a sweeping gesture
Toward the valley.
With a deep sigh he continued:
"Jest too d—n much scenery."